THE CHURCH'S
PORTRAITS
OF JESUS

He came to us as One unknown, without a name, as of old, by the lakeside. . . . And to those who obey Him, whether they be wise or simple, He will reveal Himself in the toils, the conflicts, the sufferings which they shall pass through in His fellowship, as, as an ineffable mystery, they shall learn in their own experience Who He is.

—Albert Schweitzer

The Church's Portraits of Jesus

Linda McKinnish Bridges

SMYTH & HELWYS
PUBLISHING, INC.
Macon Georgia

ISBN 1-57312-003-0

The Church's Portraits of Jesus

Linda McKinnish Bridges

Copyright © 1997
Smyth & Helwys Publishing, Inc.
6316 Peake Road
Macon, Georgia 31210-3960
1-800-747-3016

Library of Congress Cataloging-in-Publication

Bridges, Linda McKinnish.
    The church's portraits of Jesus/
    Linda McKinnish Bridges.
    viii + 120 pp.   6" x 9" (15 x 23 cm.)
    Includes bibliographical references.
    ISBN 1-57312-003-0   (alk. paper)
    1. Jesus Christ—Biography—History and criticism.
    2. Bible. N. T. Gospels—Criticism. Interpretation, etc—
    History—20th century. I. Title.
    BT301.9.875   1997
    232.9'01
    [B]—DC21   97-8701
                                                CIP

Contents

Preface

These words are from my head and from my heart. My quest for Jesus has been shaped in the classroom where academic inquiry reigns; in the sanctuary where worship is the desired goal; and in the home where loving, learning, and worship create the world of family. I am thankful for those who have cherished and also challenged my ideas.

I am thankful for the learning community at Baptist Theological Seminary at Richmond. My ideas have been shaped by hours of classroom discussions in New Testament introduction courses and various electives taught in the Gospel narratives. For seminary colleagues, especially my teacher and friend, R. Alan Culpepper, who has been a thoughtful mentor and gentle caretaker of my ideas about God, I am indebted.

The family of faith at Northminster Baptist Church in Richmond, Virginia, has nurtured my need to worship and to be in fellowship with God and people. For nine years I have worshiped in their sanctuary surrounded by beautiful portraits of Jesus etched in stained glass and seen on the faces of my sisters and brothers in Christ. I am thankful.

For my husband, Tilden, and son, Kyle, who are always providing new insights about God as we go about the daily tasks of life, I am especially grateful. They help me paint Jesus in colors that are relevant and honest to life.

I owe the greatest gratitude to my first pastor and Bible teacher, my parents, Harold and Lois McKinnish. I borrowed my first portrait of Jesus from them. Their faith, found at home and at church in identical measure, was the bedrock of my own experience of God, framing an intimate and loving portrait of Jesus.

For these communities of faith and their various portraits of Jesus Christ I am thankful. And to the Christ who has made all of these possible, glory forever and ever. Amen.

The Four Gospels
A Portrait Gallery

What did Jesus *really* look like? No matter what our age, what stage of faith maturity, how many times we have read the Bible or gone to church, all of us at some point have wondered about Jesus' physical characteristics. Did he have long flowing hair and dreamy eyes, as we have seen him portrayed in the movies? Was Jesus' hair really blonde and his eyes blue as twentieth-century paintings depict him? What was the angle of his chin, the shape of his nose? Were his facial lines from the sun, smiles, or frowns? What was his most prominent gesture? Did he really raise his hands in a sign of blessing, extending thumb and two fingers to the heavens, as Byzantine icons would have us believe? Or was he just as likely to be seen with hands and fingers wrapped around a piece of bread or a cup eating with the hungry?

We may never know how Jesus appeared in first-century Palestine. No one thought to leave a visual record of Jesus' visage. Archaeological digs have yet to uncover pieces of sculpture, sections of mosaic tile, or even fragments of wall frescos that show us the actual face of Jesus. Why not? It was not that visual representations were not popular in antiquity. It was customary to remember a great hero with many types of portraits. Heads and full figures of kings and emperors, such as Alexander the Great and Caligula, were carefully crafted in stone, some of which can be seen in art museums today. But not Jesus. As far as we know, no one thought to preserve the memory of Jesus through pictorial representation.

Perhaps it is this very absence of stone, mosaic tiles, and written description of physical characteristics that gives Jesus' authenticity. This Jesus, a radical prophet who had come to save the world, was truly an unrecognized Savior who lived not to be remembered as some king in history but to be worshiped as the Lord of all.

The Gospel writers and their communities of faith chose not to leave a pictorial representation of their Savior. Instead the communities of Matthew, Mark, Luke, and John left portraits of Jesus that move beyond information of angles of chin, hair color, and physical posture. They left us a living and dynamic art gallery of Jesus' portraits not with paint, brush, or stretched canvas, but with stories, records of conversations with Jesus and a host of folk, sermons preached by the water and on a mountain, and vivid recollections of healings and miracles.

A few years ago while flying on a commercial flight from Louisville to Atlanta, I began to explore seriously the various portraits of Jesus. On a Friday afternoon I boarded the plane, tired from a week-long speaking engagement for the Women's Missionary Union in Kentucky. I found my seat and spoke to my seatmate, a tired businessman who had just finished a major presentation and did not want to have to speak to another person until he got home. I said, Hello; he grunted. So we both settled in for a nap and some deserved solitude as the plane prepared to leave the runway.

In a few moments we reached cruising altitude. I was just beginning to sleep, when suddenly I began to sense heavy pressure in my hands and feet. I opened my eyes and saw my seatmate awake nervously looking out the window. Much to my horror, I realized that our plane was in rapid descent. I checked my watch and computed that we were not yet even halfway to Atlanta. Something was wrong. The plane was losing altitude, the cabin pressure was getting heavier, and the beverage cart had just tipped over. My once noncommunicative seatmate looked over at me as if to say, "Can't you do something?" I gasped. Just as I was trying to find some words to calm him and me as well, the oxygen masks popped out of the overhead bins. I had done some flying before, even several international flights, but never had I seen those oxygen masks, except, of course, during the cabin orientation presented by the flight attendants, which everyone ignores anyway.

The masks were flopping in our faces, and we were frozen—immobilized—thinking that this really could not be happening. The plane continued to descend. The flight attendants, no longer walking the aisles, took vacant seats in the cabin, buckled up, and began shouting instructions to us: "Take your masks, and put them on your face." I looked back, saw the fear in their faces, and heard the desperation in their voices. And I began to panic.

I leaned over to my seatmate for some help. The same man who had only minutes before had avoided even a glance from my direction, now breathing through an oxygen mask, took my hand, and with a trembling voice said, "Lady, do you know how to pray?" What goes through your mind in those few seconds when you think that you are experiencing your last moments of life? You certainly do not care that your Coke has just spilled in your lap, that your purse has rolled down the aisle, or even that you are holding hands with a complete stranger. I took his hand, as if we had been friends for life, and certainly with the keen possibility that we might be friends in death. I could not offer an audible prayer. Fear had paralyzed my vocal cords. I simply closed my eyes and tried to picture Jesus in my mind.

I know this may sound strange to you, but I actually began to image Jesus. My rationale was sound. I thought that in a few minutes I would be dying. I wanted to be able to concentrate on the physical face of Jesus so that death would be less traumatic. While trying to focus on a picture of Jesus in my mind, I thought of my wonderful husband, Tilden, and other members of our family. With sadness at leaving them and fearing what trauma might occur in the next few minutes, I closed my eyes and tried to see Jesus.

I first thought of a physical image, like the picture of Jesus that hung in the primary Sunday School class. It was Warner Sallman's *Head of Christ* that was so popular in the 1950s, portraying Jesus as a blue-eyed blonde with long wavy hair and tense facial features—the California surfer look. This picture of Jesus was printed on thousands of key-chains, kitchen calendars, and other ecclesiastical memorabilia after World War II.[1] It might have brought great comfort to soldiers in European trenches longing for home during the war, but it wasn't working for me 30,000 feet in the air. During that moment it mattered not that Jesus' hair looked bleached and dried by the sun, or that he looked like one of my hippie friends from the 60s. The need for detailed facial features faded as the reality of death became nearer. I was looking for something more than simply a pretty face. I wanted the *presence* of the One whom I had been calling "friend" for a long time; the One that I had been reading about all those years, from primary class in Sunday School to seminar room in graduate school; the One whose life I tried to follow, even now as I was returning home from a preaching assignment.

From that moment on I do not recall seeing Jesus with any physical description, although I do believe that Jesus of Nazareth was a real person with human features like the rest of us. But at that moment in time, the physical features did not matter. I remember seeing a presence of warm light, a presence beyond detailed physical attributes. I remember sensing deep companionship, a certainty that this Jesus whom I had been following all these years would be there when I made the move from life to death to life and would welcome me to my new home.

As the plane descended and I prepared to die, I closed my eyes, still clasping the hand of my neighbor. I focused on Jesus. I became calm. The plane began to level. The flight attendants left their seats and quietly began to check on passengers. My seatmate and I spoke not a word. The moment was too sacred. We were going to be okay. We took off our masks and listened as the pilot apologized for the turbulence. We had entered a wind shear. We were going to be landing in Atlanta soon. My new friend and I smiled at one another and together thanked God for life and for the skill of our pilot. We landed without any problem.

What fascinates me about this story is not necessarily the drama of the moment, although I choose not to talk about it often for I can still remember the fear. What I like to recall are my thoughts during what I thought might be my last ones on earth. I honestly searched for a picture of Jesus. I flipped through my mental files of Baptist iconography and found one hanging on the wall of my little primary Sunday School class. But in those few seconds, I discovered that the picture would not work. I needed something more than what a visual portrait could offer. I needed a picture of Jesus Christ that transcended physical attributes: Light, Presence, Companionship.

I chose a portrait of Jesus that was more like a collage than a formal portrait. My picture did not look like the portrait on the wall in Sunday School. Rather, this Jesus looked like the one I had invited into my heart because of the warmth of a Sunday School teacher and a loving family. The picture looked more like an open Bible in worship, where I could hear those old gospel stories through the preaching of the Word and the singing of the hymns. For me, Jesus' portrait was not limited simply to one artist's view of conjectured physical attributes, but was carefully drawn from the experiences of communities of faith from centuries past and from the faith experiences of my present. Like the Gospel writers and their congregations, I knew that Jesus could not be carved in stone nor stretched on canvas, but had to be drawn on the hearts and in the minds of believers.

Portraits Beyond Pictures

Webster's Dictionary defines portrait as a "pictorial representation (as a painting) of a person, usually showing one's face." The dictionary, however, adds another definition, one often ignored by patrons of visual art but carefully noted by writers. The second definition for portrait is a "graphic portrayal in words." A fine portrait does not always require canvas, brush, or paint. A portrait can simply be drawn from words. Words that are formed into sentences, then into paragraphs, and fitted into stories, have the power to etch fine, memorable portraits into the consciousness of the reader. This kind of literary portrait maintains just as much vibrancy as the visual one, sometimes even more.

Sometimes a literary portrait is superior to a visual one. Visual portraits freeze the subject(s) into a particular chronological time and geographical place. For example, the child whose portrait is painted at seven years of age in front of his toy chest will always look seven years old in the painting even when the child has become an adult and can no longer remember the toy chest. On the other hand, portraits painted with words and stories need not be limited by time or descriptions of physicality. Words contain the power to reflect more than one dimension of chronology and personality. Word pictures focus not only on outer descriptions of the subject, such as shape of nose or curve of chin, but move us inside the subject to visualize aspects of the subject's inner self, such as personality, temperament, character, and relationships to others— elements a painting does not reveal.

The Gospel narratives, likewise, move us beyond the world of physicality. In the Gospel gallery, we do not see the color of Jesus' hair nor the shape of his eyes. Rather, we see how he treated people, what he said to hungry people, to hurting people, to people living on the outside of the tradition. We see how Jesus handled crises of life and death, how he managed conflict and escalating opposition. The portraits that use words and paragraphs rather than paint and canvas give us an opportunity to view the many dimensions of Jesus' personality.

It is important, however, to remember that even in the portraits beyond visual pictures, the Gospel stories of Jesus do not ignore Jesus' humanity. We do not have a transcendent, celestial, literary portrait that neglects historical shapes. The Gospel stories tell us of a human Jesus in a given particular time frame. We learn in the four Gospels that Jesus was born of a woman; became thirsty, hungry, and tired; needed sleep as well as conversations with friends; knew anger as well as deep peace; could talk to the not-so-pretty people of society as well as to the religious elite; and was from Nazareth as well as from above.

In this same portrait gallery we see Jesus' picture painted with another perspective. Words describe Jesus' intimate thoughts, his conversations with friends and enemies, other people's evaluations of him, recorded speeches, remembered sayings, and his actions. These Gospel portraits transcend mere physical description of Jesus' face and posture, for Jesus is teacher, friend, suffering servant, and Savior of the world. These literary treasures are painted from the hearts and minds of first-century Christians who remembered Jesus not as he looked but as he spoke and acted. And these literary portraits are always current, not frozen in chronological or geographical frames.

Portraits from the Gospels

It was not easy being the first artists to draw Jesus' literary portrait. These communities of faith, who huddled around evangelists Matthew, Mark, Luke, and John, did not begin as publishing houses, but rather as small groups of people united by a common bond—the worship of Jesus. And they remembered. They remembered when they celebrated the Lord's Supper, when they ate the fellowship meal, and when they gathered to pray and worship.

Although, these Gospel communities were the first to draw literary portraits, they were not the first to remember. These writing communities were the heirs of oral stories previously told about Jesus around campfires and supper tables. Storytellers who quietly worked without leaving any paper trails kept the Jesus story alive for at least three decades or more after Jesus' death. These storytellers belonged to that faithful remnant of followers who had remained in Jerusalem (Acts 2:5-13). The gift of oral proclamation had been given to them at Pentecost. Through the years between Jesus' death and before the writing of the Gospels believers faithfully remembered the sayings of Jesus. Perhaps they even collected them, grouping the words around common themes to make the sayings of Jesus easier to remember. Some remembered Jesus' miracles, assigning them numbers as a kind of memory device. Others told the stories of Jesus' healing and compassion for people. They repeated Jesus' parables, adapting them to new audiences and new situations.

While the Jesus tradition was being remembered in various places including Palestine, Paul and other missionaries were taking the story to Asia Minor. In the middle of the first century, perhaps a decade prior to the writing of the Gospel portraits, Paul's ministry was to start churches and write letters. Although Paul does not retell the Gospel stories in his letters, the tradition of Jesus—his life, death, and resurrection—is foundational to the development of the early churches. Paul assumed in his writings that the believers knew the Gospel stories. From Paul's letters we know that the early believers met to hear the stories and to remember Jesus in synagogues, by riverbanks, and in people's homes (1 Cor 11:23-26; 15:3-11).

But then the eyewitnesses began to die. By the sixth decade of the first century, some of those eyes who had actually seen Jesus faded with death, and the voices of other believers were silenced by persecution. The church faced the awful possibility that the stories about Jesus might die with the eyewitnesses.

Something had to be done to keep these oral stories about Jesus alive. The stories had power. People heard them and encountered Christ. The church could not lose the tradition. The oral stories had to be written for others to hear. The four Gospels—Mark, Matthew, Luke, and John—emerged as literary portraits of Jesus, written between A.D. 60 and 90 to keep the oral tradition of Jesus alive.

The story of Jesus that had first been remembered by storytellers around the campfire was fixed in written form and has been on public display for more than 1,500 years. The portraits of Jesus—told by those who had actually seen, and remembered by those who had not seen yet believed—were collected and organized in a literary portrait gallery: the four Gospels.

This gallery of portraits would always be on display in the New Testament, revealing both the subject (Jesus Christ) and the artists (the ancient communities of faith).

Portraits from Artists and Biblical Scholars

The writing of the four Gospels did not signal the end of Jesus' portrait painting. Although the New Testament canon was closed, that did not stop the commissioning of additional portraits. People of all epochs and places have wanted to paint Jesus' picture. Just as the early believers drew Jesus' portrait through oral storytelling and the ancient Gospel communities painted words on parchment and papyri, communities of faith continue to add to the gallery. Even though Jesus Christ belongs historically to the world of first-century Palestine, people from other places and other eras also produce portraits of Jesus.

In Japanese art, Jesus appears as an oriental with smooth, black hair. In American films, he looks like a blonde, blue-eyed sportsman from some Ivy League university. In feminist sculpture, Jesus is portrayed as Christa, bearing physical resemblance to a woman. African artists portray Jesus with facial features belonging to an African. On Byzantine icons, Jesus is painted as the stern, bearded figure of the Pantocrator, raising his hand to bless or to judge the world. The humanity of Jesus highlighted post-Renaissance European art.

The plethora of pictures does not belong to the world of visual art alone. Biblical scholars continue to strive to paint portraits of Jesus with words. Fascinated with the quest for the historical Jesus, scholars have used reams of paper, computer disks, and stacks of books in the never-ending effort to flesh out the *real* Jesus. Some early twentieth-century scholars wanted to paint their portrait of Jesus as a radical prophet who constantly shouted, "The Kingdom has come." Other scholars wrote about Jesus as the teacher who walked around with disciples trying to teach others how to live life with a sense of ethical responsibility.

In the last twenty years, biblical scholarship has produced the following literary portraits: a political revolutionary (S. G. F. Brandon—1967), a magician (Morton Smith—1978), a Galilean charismatic (Geza Vermes—1981, 1984), a Galilean rabbi (Bruce Chilton—1984), an Essene (Henry Falk—1985), and an eschatological prophet (E. P. Sanders—1985). In 1991, two books on the historical Jesus appeared on the scene written by J. Dominic Crossan and John P. Meier who, although using different methodological tools, both portrayed Jesus as a marginalized peasant.[2] Crossan paints Jesus' portrait with these words:

> He comes as yet unknown into a hamlet of Lower Galilee. He is watched by the cold, hard eyes of peasants living long enough at a subsistence level to know exactly where the line is drawn between poverty and destitution. He looks like a beggar, yet his eyes lack the proper cringe, his voice the proper whine, his walk the proper shuffle. He speaks about the rule of God, and they listen as much from curiosity as anything else.[3]

Meier draws his portrait of Jesus in this way:

> Jesus, the poor layman turned prophet and teacher, the religious figure from rural Galilee without credentials, met his death in Jerusalem . . . a poor layman from the Galilean hillside with disturbing doctrines and claims was marginal both in the sense of being dangerously antiestablishment and in the sense of lacking a power base in the capital. He could easily be brushed aside into the dustbin of death.[4]

And we ask ourselves, was Jesus a political revolutionary or an eschatological prophet? Was Jesus a Galilean rabbi or a marginalized peasant? Will the real Jesus please stand up? How does one compare the variations of tint and shades of light in all of these portraits? Which portrait deserves the best and central location in the gallery? What does it mean that one subject can have so many different interpretations?

The Art of Portraiture

And we continue to ask: What does Jesus really look like? To American scholars writing in the political turmoil of the Vietnam War era where an antiestablishment mentality was in vogue, Jesus appears as a political revolutionary. To scholars writing during the extreme economic polarities of the modern 1990s where rich get richer and poor get poorer, where society makes decisions on political expediency and economic security, Jesus appears as a marginalized peasant. These portraits are painted with a literary paintbrush dipped in the palette of personal and cultural contextualization. Whether it be the soft face of Sallman's blue-eyed Jesus that became an icon of paternalistic piety for homesick boys during the war, or the Jesus standing with the poor and the disenfranchised drawn by Catholic scholars concerned for social justice, we tend to draw pictures of Jesus that reveal the posture of the painter. In other words, the portraits of Jesus not only describe Jesus, but also resemble the ones doing the painting.

What does all of this mean? Does this mean that Jesus is simply a figment of our cultural imagination, or a simple reflection of whatever ideological convention appears to be in vogue at that time? The complexity and simplicity of portrait drawing demand our attention. The broader issue deals with the process of interpretation. An even larger question deals with the production of meaning. How is meaning produced? What happens to us when we view fine art? What processes are used to create interpretations? How much influence does the artist have on the portrait? What about the artist's community? How are they involved? How do we interpret Jesus' portraits in the four Gospels?

An example from the world of visual art illustrates the process. Artist Ephraim Rubenstein, professor at the University of Richmond, paints beautiful visual responses to literary texts. His most recent exhibit featured paintings inspired by the poetry of Rainer Maria Rilke, a German poet writing in the early twentieth century. As I entered the University's art gallery one afternoon, I recognized the forces at work in

11

Rubenstein's productions. Each painting had sections of Rilke's writing attached to various corners; Rubenstein loves Rilke's poetry. Each painting depicted scenes from the James River; Rubenstein also loves the James, that scenic waterway that runs through the city of Richmond and not far from Rubenstein's home. But how did all of those "loves" connect to produce the visual drama I saw stretched on pieces of canvas in the gallery that day?

The process is simple yet so very complex. A young artist from Brooklyn, New York, paints visual responses, using scenes from a river in Richmond, Virginia, to literary texts belonging to an early twentieth-century German poet whom the artist Rubenstein has never met. The forces between text and context converged beautifully in Rubenstein's exhibit.

In a phone conversation, I asked Rubenstein how he did it, how he made all those forces come together. Did he read the text first and then go sit by the James River? Or did he sit by the river and then read Rilke's poetry? After a long silence, he said that he read Rilke's poetry for so many months that the text actually lived in his mind and heart. He thought constantly of visual responses to Rilke's written words. He adopted a Rilkian way of thinking, seeing life from the poet's perspective. In the process his own present environment, a southern riverbank, became a backdrop for communicating German poetry. It works. See Rubenstein's work, and you hear Rilke. See Rubenstein, and you see the James River. The subject, Rilke's writings, became a part of the artist. And the context, the James River, became the channel of communication. The subject and the context work to produce meaning.

But wait a minute, there is more to the production of meaning than just text and context. The literary text of Rilke's German poetry was displayed in scenes from Rubenstein's context, the James River. And meaning was produced, or was it? Meaning, at least for me, did not occur until I walked into the University's art gallery and studied Rubenstein's work. It was at that moment, as I stood in front of each painting, recalling some of my own reading from Rilke and remembering my own experiences on the James River, that meaning occurred. I was crucial to the interpretation process. Text communicated through contexts makes sense only when a viewer brings his or her own context to the painting.

How does all of this work for understanding the portraits of Jesus? The text of the Gospel portraits is Jesus Christ. The context belongs to the social worlds of the four communities of faith. And you and I are the readers. All three forces—text, context, and readers—are at work in the portrait gallery. We see the portraits of Jesus. We also see the pictures of four communities of faith as they viewed the portraits of Jesus. And we see ourselves as we watch the ancient communities of faith portray Jesus.

In that process of portraiture, the Holy Spirit works to provide the images, the colors, the shades of lighting, and the visual perception. We see because the Holy Spirit guides us to see both the picture of Jesus and those of others and ourselves. The art of portraiture in the Gospel narratives is not a random event but the work of the Spirit who teaches us how to remember, how to see, and then guides us to believe (John 14:26).

The Text—Jesus of Nazareth

Jesus is the text, or the subject, of the Gospel portraits. Granted, we do not have a large supply of historical data, but from various sources, both extracanonical and canonical, we know that Jesus lived. For example, Josephus, Jewish aristocrat and historian of the first century, writes this about Jesus in his *Jewish Antiquities:*

> At this time there appeared Jesus, a wise man, if indeed one should call him a man. For he was a doer of startling deeds, a teacher of people who received truth with pleasure. And he gained a following both among many Jews and among many of Greek origin. He was the Messiah. And when Pilate, because of an accusation made by the leading men among us, condemned him to the cross, those who had loved him previously did not cease to do so.[5]

13

Other writers of the first century also mention Jesus, such as Suetonius, Pliny the Younger, and Lucian. But our information about Jesus Christ comes primarily through the first four books in the New Testament—Matthew, Mark, Luke, and John. These evangelists chose to collect pieces of oral tradition about Jesus and to organize them into written portraits. As they collected the oral stories, they remembered Jesus in the context of their own community crises and traumas. As a result, Jesus' portrait shines in memorial to Jesus Christ and gives us a view of the ancient church's communities as they remembered Jesus.

The Context—The Four Communities

Some scholars think the Gospels were written by individual evangelists. Certainly, someone took the responsibility of writing the document in its final form. But what I want to emphasize here is not the fine achievements of individuals, but the work of communities of believers who helped shape these Gospels and, in turn, were shaped by them.

The words of Jesus permeated the minds and hearts of the evangelists and their communities of faith. The words of Jesus rang in their ears as they lived their first-century Mediterranean lives. The sayings of Jesus, the miracles, the death and resurrection stories—all were a part of their consciousness. These stories did not fade into the background when the community was faced with a particular problem. Rather, the stories surfaced from their memory banks and became a part of their world. The stories of Jesus interfaced with their own personal stories.

In the process of interpretation, the subject becomes part of the context, and the context becomes a part of the subject. For example, it was comforting for these ancient communities to remember Jesus' words about persecution while they were experiencing abuse from the government thirty years after Jesus' own death. To hear Jesus speak against the religious tradition in the third decade of the first century had particular meaning for the church facing expulsion from the Jewish

14

synagogue in the 70s. The church remembered Jesus because they needed help for their lives at that moment. And as they remembered, their picture of Jesus looked not only like Jesus Christ but also like them. Like the artist Rubenstein who paints pictures from literary texts by placing them in his own contemporary context, the four communities painted pictures of Jesus in the context of their own individual personalities, community crises, and views of the world. Portraits, therefore, not only portray subjects; they also reveal artists.

The Reader—You and Me

To close the hermeneutical circle with a nice analysis of the portraits of Jesus and the communities who painted them is not enough. The production of meaning is not that simple. Even though we isolate Jesus' portraits and present a careful sociological analysis of the communities of faith, we still cannot say we understand the meaning of Jesus in the four Gospels.

Meaning involves the text, context, and the reader. The reader will always have the first and the final word. The process of understanding biblical texts is dialogical, constantly moving back and forth from text to context, context to text, and always in continuous dialogue with the reader. *I* chose to view Rubenstein's paintings in the gallery. *I* also interpreted his work in light of my own experiences with the James River and Rilke's poetry. Art interpretation, fortunately, has traditionally given the viewer much freedom of interpretation, highlighting the subjectivity of art.

Biblical interpretation as developed by the academy has not always been as generous. Readers are often viewed as silent, passive observers with the potential to sabotage, rather than produce, meaning. Therefore, the commentator, usually white and male, serves as the sole authority for meaning of biblical texts. Some scholars assumed that readers only brought misleading subjectivity to the highly-objective and scientific task of biblical interpretation. Recent scholarly work, however, has begun to refute this position.

15

A few years ago, I visited a women's Sunday School class in a small Baptist church deep in the mountains of North Carolina. The class, made up of mountain grandmothers with hands aged by hard work and minds sharpened by life experiences, sat around a long table with open Bibles. The teacher, the one who had the quarterly, quickly introduced the lesson. Then she stopped. Everyone but I knew what was to happen next. Like clockwork, the exegetical circle began. The woman at the end of the table began to "expound" on the lesson passage, explaining what the verses had meant to her during the death of her only son. Unable to speak because of her tears, the next woman touched the arm of the woman beside her, indicating her pass. Another woman described the significance of the passage in her life as she faced a terminal illness. Women sitting around the table during the Sunday School hour with their opened Bibles and shared life experiences were just as involved in the production of meaning as the finest exegetical, commentary treatment of that particular passage. Not one woman around the table knew biblical Greek nor the ancient customs of the Mediterranean world. They were not conversant with redaction or form criticism. Yet they were interpreting scripture. Using their own life experiences and the biblical text, they were producing meaning.

A new look at how we understand the Bible positions the reader in the center of the hermeneutical process. You and I come to the portraits of Jesus with preconceived notions of Jesus' identity that shape our reading. As we actively read, we are also constantly being shaped by our reading. Old notions are challenged or confirmed; new understandings are added. This dialogic movement cannot be ignored.

This book, therefore, will not be complete until you have interacted with this material and have found something that makes a difference in your life. As you read this book, observe the particular colors used by the communities of faith to paint the portrait of Jesus. Notice carefully their particular perspective and their choice of canvas. Watch the followers of Jesus as they hear the comforting words of their Savior speak to their daily frustrations of political and religious isolation. Then we, too, will see a Jesus who wants to reside in *our* hearts and minds, not just in the crevices of an ancient literary text.

The portraits of Jesus were not designed to be placed in a remote art gallery far from the main avenue of life experiences. They are to be placed in the middle of our everyday lives. We read the Bible because we see ourselves in its pages, and then we know how to live. We learn from those ancient characters how to shape our lives in relationship to Jesus Christ. The portraits of Jesus left by the communities of faith help us, as twentieth-century followers of Jesus, design our own portrait. Because of this first-century context, its ancient literary product, and the power of the Holy Spirit, we bring our own experiences to our reading of these Gospel narratives, knowing that in our reading we are likely to be transformed. Enter the art gallery now with all of your senses alert. Acknowledge your own presuppositions regarding former understandings of Jesus. See again the portraits of Jesus, the pictures of the communities who produced the portraits. While you are reading, watch the words become small mirrors reflecting your own image and the image of what you can become in Jesus Christ.

Notes

[1]David Morgan, "Sallman's *Head of Christ:* The History of an Image," *Christian Century,* 109 (7 October 1992): 868-70.

[2]John P. Meier, *A Marginal Jew: Rethinking the Historical Jesus* (New York: Doubleday, 1991); and J. D. Crossan, *The Historical Jesus: The Life of a Mediterranean Jewish Peasant* (San Francisco: Harper, 1991).

[3]Crossan, xi.

[4]Meier, 9.

[5]Josephus, *Jewish Antiquities* 18.3. par. 63-64, Loeb Classical Library (Cambridge MA: Harvard University Press, 1930).

For Further Reading

Anderson, Hugh, ed. *Jesus.* Englewood Cliffs NJ: Prentice-Hall, 1967.

Beuchner, Frederick and Lee Botlin, photography. *Faces of Jesus.* New York: Riverwood Publishers, 1974.

Kee, Howard Clark. *What Can We Know About Jesus?* Cambridge MA: Cambridge University Press, 1990.

Kingsbury, Jack Dean. *Jesus Christ in Matthew, Mark, and Luke.* Proclamation Commentary. Philadelphia: Fortress Press, 1981.

Muggeridge, Malcolm. *Jesus Rediscovered.* Garden City NY: Doubleday, 1979.

Wilson, A. N. *Jesus: A Life.* New York: Fawcett Columbine, 1992.

Chapter 1

The Portrait of Jesus
in Mark

Have you ever walked into a room and known immediately that a loved one had just left? You saw signs of her presence everywhere—the impression of her head against the cushion, her favorite book on the floor, a glass half empty by the chair, her perfume still in the air. Reading the Gospel of Mark gives that same sensation—that Jesus has just left and that you have just missed seeing him in person. It is almost as though you have run down to the shore to catch the boat to be near him, but the boat has left the dock only moments earlier. As you stand there on the beach, you can see the waves from the wake of the boat breaking on the sand. You notice footprints along the shore line. As you walk, you discover a half-eaten loaf of bread reminding you that Jesus was here just a few moments ago.

The First Portrait

Perhaps the reason Jesus seems so close in the Gospel of Mark is because this Gospel is the first literary portrait of Christ. The community of Mark's Gospel wrote their memories of Jesus before any of the other communities. You may wonder how this can be since Matthew actually appears first in the New Testament canon. The placement of the Gospels in the New Testament is not chronological. Scholars, carefully researching the literary relationships between the four

Gospels, suggest that Mark was written first, sometime in the late 60s or early 70s, using material from the oral tradition accumulated after Jesus' death. Matthew and Luke were written next. The precise date is difficult to establish, but it was sometime in the early to middle 80s. Matthew and Luke used Mark as a source, along with other sources no longer available to us. The last Gospel to be written was John, the final edition developed in the 90s. The community of John's Gospel may have known of the sources behind Mark, Matthew, and Luke but also chose to use additional sources.

While the four Gospels cannot be harmonized into one account, similar material can be found in all four Gospels. Areas of disagreement also must be given careful attention. In these places of disagreement, the individual concerns of the Gospel community are clearly seen. You can do this careful research for yourself. Sit down with a New Testament that arranges the four Gospels into parallel columns; then compare and contrast the material found in the four accounts. You will be surprised at what you will find.

The Gospels share similar features in that they all give a portrait of Jesus with the same basic outline—his life, death, and resurrection. Yet each Gospel paints the portrait in a different manner, with different colors and shading. Notice the similarities between the stories of Jesus' baptism in Matthew 3:13-17; Mark 1:9-11; Luke 3:21-22; and John 1:29-34. Similarities can also be seen in the four accounts of the cleansing of the temple in Matthew 21:12-13; Mark 11:15-17; Luke 19:45-4; and John 2:14-22.

While you are noting the similarities, you will also observe dissimilarities. Two of the most obvious dissimilarities are found at the beginning and ending of each of the Gospels. For example, read Mark's abrupt introduction: "The beginning of the good news of Jesus Christ, the Son of God." Compare it with the elaborate beginning of the Gospel of John: "In the beginning was the Word, and the Word was with God, and the Word was God."

In contrast, Matthew uses a complex genealogical discussion to show that Jesus is related to David and Abraham. Luke, on the other hand, offers an extended, formal beginning with painstaking attention to detail:

> Since many have undertaken to set down an orderly account of the events that have been fulfilled among us, just as they were handed on to us by those who from the beginning were eyewitnesses.

Observe the dissimilarities of the endings of the Gospel narratives. The oldest manuscripts of Mark's Gospel conclude at 16:8, where frightened women leave an empty tomb. In contrast, Matthew closes with the disciples on a mountain with the resurrected Jesus receiving instructions for the future (Matt 28:16-20). Luke, on the other hand, wants the reader to know that Jesus not only has been resurrected but has returned to God in the presence of joyous disciples (Luke 24:50-53). John ends with a literary epilogue designed to convince the reader that the story of Jesus has been received from the beloved disciple and is reliable.

How are these stories related? What is their literary history? Our conclusions remain tentative. We do not have access to the minds of these ancient writers nor dates of composition. We can surmise, however, that Mark may have been the first Gospel to have been written, serving as the literary base for the other Gospels. For it appears that Matthew and Luke borrowed almost 90 percent of Mark's account and tried to improve Mark's rustic Greek grammar. Another source, called Q (from the German word *Quelle*, translated "source"), may have also influenced the formation of Matthew and Luke, especially the sayings and teachings of Jesus not found in Mark. John knew of the Markan source although he did not copy it as closely as Matthew and Luke.

Bear in mind, however, that these literary relationships are merely conjectures. No dates of original composition have been found, even on the earliest manuscripts. We cannot outline with full confidence the literary relationship between all four Gospels. We can, however, carefully observe their uniformity and diversity in this amazing gallery of Jesus' portraits. We can view each individual portrait as a unique contribution of the Gospel community, seeing a clear portrait of Jesus and the community who remembered him. More importantly, in the Gospel gallery we can also see ourselves and our relationship to Jesus.

Jesus' Portrait

What does Jesus look like in Mark's Gospel? In Mark, Jesus is preacher, healer, teacher, traveler, miracle worker, and always moving quickly from one place to another. You get the sense from reading Mark that Jesus has so much to do in such a little time. The reader stays alert watching the frantic pace of Jesus and the disciples. Notice the frequent use of the word "immediately" in chapter 1 alone (vv. 12, 18, 20, 21, 29, 42). We watch Jesus travel—moving from one side of the sea to the other (4:35; 5:1; 5:21; 6:45; 6:53). Jesus leaves the Gentile side of the lake to arrive on the other side, the Jewish territory, and then goes back again. He travels to make an important theological point—that God has come for both Jew and Gentile.

Mark's portrait comes in multiple hues and colors. Yet two significant brush strokes should be noted. On one hand, Jesus is powerful, able to heal diseases, calm storms, walk on water, and openly defy religious authorities. On the other hand, Jesus suffers and painfully endures isolation, ridicule from family and friends, and ultimately death. These two contrasting portraits of power and weakness are painted simultaneously in Mark's Gospel. Mark's portrait of Jesus is much like an optical illusion—like those seen carved on a piece of wood that spell the name "Jesus." Lines are etched to create a picture, although at first glance all you see is a haphazard presentation of intersecting lines. You focus on the lines for a moment, then a picture appears, and the random lines disappear. The myriad of lines is replaced with a recognizable configuration—Jesus.

In Mark's Gospel, the first and most obvious lines paint a picture of Jesus as strong, powerful, able to subdue nature and disease. At second glance, however, Jesus appears weak, passive, impotent, prone more to suffer than to exhibit power. In Mark, Jesus is like a mighty roaring lion who, although king of the jungle, falls passively to packs of predators. The two pictures of power and pain are painted with contrasting colors chosen from opposite sides of the color wheel and form a composite portrait of Jesus Christ as one who is all powerful and yet suffers greatly. These two portraits might appear contradictory at first, like the disconnected lines of an optical illusion. In the final glance, however, the picture is clear and distinct. You can recognize that Jesus is the Son of God.

Jesus' Power

Members of Mark's community of faith could have just as well used fireworks or some other brilliant display of majesty and power when they painted Jesus' portrait in the first seven chapters of Mark's Gospel. The pyrotechnics of this Gospel are not understated. Jesus bursts on the scene in the first chapter, first verse with this abrupt Markan proclamation: "The beginning of the good news of Jesus Christ, the Son of God." No soft, muted, pastel tones are in the color palette here. Bold, bright primary colors are used to announce that Jesus, God's Son, is on the scene. Like a trumpeter standing on the tallest tower in the fortressed city declaring that the army has just defeated the closest enemy and victory is assured, Jesus is here, the Gospel says, and all is well. And the portrait begins to unfold.

This Jesus needs no sweet, romantic birth announcement to announce his arrival. Jesus' portrait in Mark omits lowly manger scenes and adolescent temple visits and begins immediately with an adult baptism (1:9-11). Then without pause, after the baptism, Jesus is driven by the Spirit into the wilderness to be tempted by the Devil (1:12-13). If you want to read the chilling details of the temptation story, you will have to go to Luke's portrait (Luke 4:14ff.), for Mark has no intention of painting the weaknesses of Jesus so boldly. Jesus starts right to work, preaching a short, succinct message, "The time is fulfilled, and the kingdom of God has come near; repent, and believe in the good news" (Mark 1:14).

When Jesus speaks, people listen and respond—even rough, earthy disciples who at Jesus' mere words leave their fish and their fathers to follow Jesus (1:16-20). Not only rough fishermen, but even the learned scribes and faithful worshipers in the synagogue recognize his power. The greatest display, more stupendous than fishermen or even scribes, is when "with authority he commands even the unclean spirits, and they obey him" (1:27).

Jesus' power also cures diseases and gives life to the lifeless. Simon's mother-in-law knows Jesus' authority (1:29-31), as does the leper (1:40-45). Jesus' authority is so powerful that it must remain clandestine. Unleashed, this power would result in Jesus' untimely death (1:43). The paralytic stretched out on a stretcher sliding down through a hole in the roof also knows that Jesus has authority (2:1-12). Even the crowds who see Jesus heal the man respond by saying, "We never saw anything like this" (2:12).

But there is more to Jesus' power. Not only can Jesus speak and heal with authority, he can also defy established religious structures. The Markan picture of Jesus uses three classical scenes to depict Jesus' authority over religious structures: Jesus eats with the disenfranchised (2:15-17), refuses to obey the fasting laws (2:18-22), and gathers grain on the Sabbath (2:23-28). This Jesus is a renegade, and he gets away with it, for a while.

How dare Jesus break with the stately religious traditions! Food laws are important, and one must always be careful to eat the right food with the right people, according to the tradition of the Jewish ancestors. This bold, maverick Jesus acts as if he has never heard of the religious laws before and defiantly challenges the system. And that is power!

Jesus' preaching has authority. His stories look simple at first glance, yet with a second look contain life-changing power with innocent images of seed and soil, faith and fruit (4:1-32). Jesus says that a seed planted in good soil has the capacity to reproduce itself a hundredfold at maturity. Furthermore, even a mature mustard seed can explode with power and provide a home for the birds of the air and a point of faith for weary, powerless listeners. This potent, parabolic language underscores Jesus' authority.

In the first four chapters of Mark, Jesus exhibits power and authority before the eyes of Jewish beholders. In chapter 5, Jesus goes to "the other side of the sea" (5:1). Now the Gentiles have an opportunity to hear and see Jesus' power. Jesus has already exhibited his power to exorcise demons for the Jews in Capernaum (1:21-28); now Jesus shows his authority by casting out demons in the Gentile country of the Gerasenes (5:1-20). This stupendous display of authority over unclean spirits receives acclaim from the crowds: "And every one was amazed" (5:20b). Back to the other side of the sea, into Jewish territory again, Jesus approaches the zenith of his powerful displays—he brings a dead, twelve-year-old girl back to life and reinstates a bleeding, unclean, marginalized woman into her religious tradition (5:21-43). These two sandwiched stories give further evidence to Jesus' power.

Our picture of Jesus is of one who says the right things, does the right things, with control over nature, disease, and religious tradition—at least until chapter 6. Here in the scene in Nazareth, with his own people—perhaps cousins, aunts, and uncles—within the familiar walls of his own synagogue, the one who seems so in control—able to heal the sick, raise the dead, subdue nature, defy tradition—becomes impotent against his opposition. This scene foreshadows the pain of the cross to come. This one who has given such a marvelous display of supernatural feats in the first half of the Gospel cannot even lead his own people to belief: "And he could do no deed of power there, except that he laid his hands on a few sick people and cured them. And he was amazed at their unbelief" (6:5-6).

Where has the power gone? Mark's portrait begins to lose symmetry here. The one with authority now gives over his authority to the disciples (6:7). In addition, the portrait of Jesus' power is temporarily overshadowed by the account of

John the Baptist's death (6:14-29). If this could happen to the popular John the Baptist, could the same end be in store for the mighty Jesus?

The interlude that questions Jesus' power is short. In chapters 6–8, Jesus miraculously feeds thousands of people twice—one feeding for the Jews (6:30-44) and another for the Gentiles (8:1-10). He walks on water (6:45-51) and heals a blind man (8:22-26). Questions, however, quietly haunt the narrative. In this grand show of strength, many still do not understand (6:52; 7:18; 8:11-13; 8:21). How can it be that this one who can convince demons to flee, waves to still, and disease to vanish cannot even persuade people to believe?

Mark's portrait of Jesus makes a major shift in the following pages. Missing will be the confident tint of the portrait where Jesus is always traveling, always healing, always teaching, and always gathering a crowd of interested observers who are eager to see a new display of power. In the following chapters, beginning in chapter 8 and continuing to the end of the narrative, the action slows. Jesus becomes quieter, more passive, more human. Another portrait of Christ is unveiled. This picture loses the magnificent fireworks of Jesus as the powerful one and paints a dark, gloomy picture of pain, blood, suffering, and death. The portrait of Jesus' power turns quickly into a portrait of Jesus' pain.

Jesus' Pain

Like the optical illusion that couches the word "Jesus" in intersecting lines and curves, Mark's narrative has provided a literary illusion. At first glance, Jesus is mighty. No one can doubt his power. At the same time he is encased in those mighty acts of supernatural feats, we watch Jesus experience pain and death in Mark's story. The intersecting lines of Jesus' power fade from sight as we see Jesus' pain. This Gospel wants us to feel that paradox and wrestle with definitions of power and pain for ourselves as we read. We can, therefore, expect that the portrait of pain will be just as graphic as the Gospel's portrait of Jesus' power.

This portrait of pain must be painted because, in Mark, to do the will of God is to suffer. Sharyn Dowd, New Testament scholar, observes that the theme of suffering is not limited to the last half of Mark's Gospel but is actually seen from the beginning, when in Mark 3:6 we learn that the Pharisees are out to destroy Jesus.[1] The concentration on pain, however, comes most vividly in 8:31, 9:30-31, and 10:33-34. Jesus makes three passion predictions in an effort to convince the disciples that he is going to suffer.

In 8:31, Jesus says "that the Son of Man must undergo great suffering, and be rejected by the elders, the chief priests, and the scribes, and be killed, and after three days rise again." The disciples are listening. Jesus' pain becomes tangible as he seems to be saying to them, "Come on fellows, help me. The going will be a little rough soon, and I am going to need some support. Can I count on you?" Yet Peter rebukes him (8:32). Clearly, the disciples do not understand. Then Jesus begins a long monologue describing what it means to suffer: "If any want to become my followers, let them deny themselves and take up their cross and follow me" (8:34) The shadow of the cross falls over the narrative here, foreshadowing the scene to come, for Jesus defines life for the follower as one who carries the cross. Suffering, pain, and perhaps death are inevitable for the followers of Christ.

In 9:31, Jesus again tries to gain a hearing. He has just healed a boy with an unclean spirit. The disciples are there to see it. After the healing Jesus begins to teach them that "the Son of Man is to be betrayed into human hands, and they will kill him"(9:30-33). Again, the disciples do not understand. After Jesus has tried to elicit their understanding and support for the rough days ahead, they begin arguing over who was the greatest among them. How can their conversations be directed in such shallow ways, when their Friend and Teacher has just opened his heart to them? They simply do not get it. Jesus is going to suffer, and they cannot even imagine the impending pain.

Another scene depicts Jesus and the disciples walking on the road to Jerusalem. Jesus knows what is about to happen. He is looking for some co-laborers. So he says again, "Hey, guys, you are still not getting the message here. Listen one more time—this time with some of the gory detail." This is Jesus' last prediction of his death—a futile effort to penetrate the thick heads of the disciples. So he says,

> See, we are going up to Jerusalem, and the Son of Man will be handed over to the chief priests and the scribes, and they will condemn him to death; and they will hand him over to the Gentiles; they will mock him, and spit upon him, and flog him, and kill him; and after three days he will rise again. (10:33-34)

The details are there; the fear is there; and Jesus, the powerful Son of God, is about to show the disciples that to follow God means to endure pain.

As we have begun to expect, the facial expressions of the disciples do not change. Their thoughts have been elsewhere as Jesus has been pouring his heart out to them. This time, the response to Jesus' plea for support is to ask for a special seat in the new Kingdom. How inconsiderate! How cold! It is like telling someone the most painful part of your life story and, while you wait for a response of support and understanding, they look at your watch and ask, "What time is it?"

These three stories paint graphic scenes of pain, not only of future gloom but of present fear and isolation. Jesus has opened his life to his disciples, and they have chosen to ignore him. It hurts, but there is more to come.

Perhaps the Gethsamene scene is the most wrenching. There we see with our own eyes and hear with our own ears the deep personal pain of Christ. It hurts to give over self to the higher purpose of God, and Jesus feels it. It is not easy, even for Jesus. In Mark 14:36, Jesus seems to say, "Abba, Father, for you all things are possible; remove this cup from me. Is there any way that I can detour from the next path? Or maybe we can start all over and leave this part out?" After the moments of wrestling with God over his future destiny, watch Jesus' back begin to straighten, his chin find definition, and his voice become lowered and calm. With resolve, Jesus seems to say, "Okay this is not about what I want; this is about what you want. Let it be done."

The wheels of pain drive on. The next scene is Jesus on the cross. Mark's Gospel leaves no doubt that Jesus Christ suffered. Hear the painful scream in 15:34—the piercing cry of dereliction that sends shivers up your spine. You can hear this expensive gospel being purchased with blood, water, and sacrifice when Jesus cries out in pain, "My God, why have you forsaken me?" And the earth becomes dark. Jesus is alone. Everyone has gone, even God. And Jesus dies.

It is not a pretty picture. Where is Sallman's blonde-haired, blue-eyed Jesus when you need him? The community of Mark's Gospel paints Jesus' face in pain, feeling rejection. The other Gospels do not ignore this attribute of Jesus; all four stories give us the harsh realities of Jesus' crucifixion and death, but none like Mark. In this Gospel, we can almost smell the suffering.

The Portrait of the Community

The portrait of Jesus in Mark has a contorted face, a bloody body, and a broken heart. This rejected Jesus has died on the cross. Even glorious resurrection day has been subdued by a narrative that closes in the silence of an empty tomb and a cemetery where the mourners have fled (16:8). It is a sad portrait. Why? If the theory of art portraiture is correct, then any painting will always leave the imprint of the artist. Someone had to choose the particular colors and the unusual shape of the story. Why did the community paint such a portrait? What problems and concerns prompted such a sad portrait of Christ?

It is important to look at the community that shaped this Gospel. The author of this Gospel is not simply a lone-ranger evangelist working in an ivory tower painting literary pictures with words in hopes that his or her name will appear in lights some day. No, this Gospel is a real-live document written for real-live people by real-live people who had real-live needs. It was the church—a real-live congregation. This Gospel was written because this story said something important to the church—those first-century believers. The Gospel of Mark was written, collected, and added to the New Testament canon because it spoke to the struggles of the Markan church and to the real-life concerns of later believers.

Let me illustrate. Imagine that four people see the same car accident from different places on the street. All four observers report the accident to you. You hear the same basic story—almost. But if you listen closely, you will actually hear four variations of the same story. Perhaps one of the eyewitnesses is a young mother. She might make her report focusing on the trauma of the young children who were not wearing seat belts in the back. Another eyewitness, a car mechanic, might describe the scene of the accident in graphic detail, noting the roar of the engine and the screech of the tires as the cars collided. A third witness, perhaps a newspaper reporter, might observe the details of the cars involved—license plates, color, and so on. And yet another witness, a state patrolman, might tell you the story describing the speed and possible traffic violations. With each account, the same story of the car accident is told with a slightly different perspective, depending on the vocation and particular interests of the teller. It is not that the witnesses disregarded the facts of the story; they simply tell you what *they* saw from *their* perspective. Consequently, you actually hear two stories—one about the car wreck and another about the observer.

We read the story of Jesus in Mark's Gospel, and we also hear the story of the community that shaped the story. Persons of the church community surrounding the Gospel of Mark were still concerned about what Jesus said and did. They did not distort the facts so that they could write an autobiography. It was not that simple. When we read their story, we can still see traces of Jesus of Nazareth. The stories of Jesus, however, were interpreted in light of their own circumstances. When we see Jesus' portrait in Mark's Gospel, we are also viewing a picture of Mark's church. A close reading of the Gospel will identify them, and we will be able to see their hopes and struggles.

We interpret history not simply in the original frame of time but from our own social location, worldview, and personal experiences. The Markan community living in the late 60s interpreted the stories of Jesus not only as they were heard in the milieu of Jesus' life, but as they were lived out in the context of life some thirty years later. Let me illustrate with a contemporary analogy.

We live in Mechanicsville, Virginia—actually in Cold Harbor of Hanover County. For those of you who know Civil War history, you know that the Seven Days Battle at Cold Harbor was the site of one of the war's bloodiest battles. Our seven-year-old son, Kyle, is fascinated by all the history surrounding him. When we moved to Cold Harbor, I must confess I could not name the war leaders—Hill, Stuart, Grant, and Sherman—or tell the stories surrounding them. Yet, Kyle plays daily in the Chickahominy battlefield. As we ride to school, we see historical markers and monuments reminding us of this period of history.

As a young fellow, Kyle is just now waking up to his outside world, looking for new heroes, exploring life beyond his backyard. And he has found these things in his love for Civil War history. History has come alive. We read, go to the parks, see the reenactors. The characters are not simply distant names in some musty history book. They are real. In the summers he pretends he can even hear the soldiers in our backyard. We sit on the front porch and try to imagine what it must have been like to have been on this property in June of 1862. Kyle feels as if he knows Robert E. Lee and General Armstrong Custer personally. These stories have meaning for him as a young fellow trying to learn about the world around him. He needs to know them and to keep their memory alive. His context demands it, so he repeats the tradition and tells the stories of gallant battles and not-so-gallant ones to our visitors. His context, both his developmental needs and our geographical location, demands that he keep these stories alive. They are a part of his world.

The Suffering Community

And so it was with persons of the church community around Mark's Gospel. Their context demanded that they keep the stories of Jesus alive. The stories of Jesus were not just facts about a musty hero of yore. This was the story of Jesus that brought meaning into their daily lives. These stories helped them make sense of who they were and where they were going. These Jesus stories were consumed by the community of believers and became their own life stories.

Who were they? When were they writing? What were their life struggles? What were they saying about themselves as they composed this first Gospel? Determining the social setting of the Gospel is not easy. Remember that we have no signed or dated manuscripts. We have no external evidence to supply corroboration. Our only source is the Gospel of Mark. We read the Gospel like an ancient palimpsest—a kind of manuscript that has two layers of written text from different periods of time. Barely distinguishable is the first layer. It has been erased to make room for another layer of text, in order to conserve expensive parchment. The top layer is much easier to read, of course. But the reader who wants to read the earlier layers must do so carefully with fine microscopic eyes, reading between the lines of the most recent edition.

The Gospel of Mark, likewise, has two layers. The first and oldest layer belongs to the tradition about Jesus. But the second layer is the story of the community. Through their choice and strategic placement of stories we can also read the top layer and learn about the church community.

We read the Gospel of Mark to answer the first question: Who were they? Scholars are divided about when and where this Gospel was written and by whom. Some suggest that Mark was written in Rome by a Jewish author for a Gentile audience. The literary evidence used to support this theory is the frequent use of Latin words, such as *modius* (4:21), *praetorium* (15:16), *centurio* (15:39), and others. Church members living in Rome would have been familiar with Latin and would have understood these words without translation.

Second, when were they writing? Perhaps they wrote in the last part of the 60s during the political reign of Nero and Vespasian. Third, what were some of their life struggles? If they were located in Rome during the late 60s, many in the community would have had to contend with grave political and economic problems prior to the war.

Recently, however, some scholars have suggested that Mark was produced in the agrarian culture of Palestine, not in a city like Rome. While the proposed date is still in the late 60s, the focus is not on a group of church members living in the city but members who live in the countryside of Palestine and face particular social problems related to their location.[2]

Scholar Chad Meyers suggests that the church community of Mark's Gospel experienced persecution from two important cultural institutions—religion and politics.[3] On the one hand, the church suffered abuse from the religious power structure. The church was experiencing strong antagonism against the entire Jerusalem system. The Jewish elders with their nobility had been given positions of authority by the Romans, and the church felt oppressed by the religious leaders. The community of Mark's Gospel uses explosive revolutionary words to ventilate its own anger at the religious establishment.

The church bears prophetic witness against the injustices and arrogance of the religious system. With a parable of the vineyard, Jesus vehemently attacks the leaders of Israel (Mark 12). The rulers are deaf and blind to the message of the prophets whom they murder. They are mere tenants and will be brutally punished for their insubordination by the true owner. God will come and destroy the tenants and give the vineyard to others. Thirty years later, the congregation uses these same words to speak to Jerusalem. The community says to the religious authorities that they should be the servants, but instead they pretend to own the vineyard. So their end is doomed. These are revolutionary words used by a single congregation directed toward an entire religious institution.

The church, on the other side, experiences abuse from Roman imperialism. Conditions are such that the Gospel cannot speak as overtly against the government as they are able to speak against the Jerusalem hierarchy. Discourse against the government must, therefore, be covert and cryptic. In veiled language, the community alludes to the necessary cleansing of the Roman government in the healing of the demoniac story (5:1-20). In this story Jesus asks the demon to reveal his identity. He replies, "My name is Legion; for we are many. He begged him earnestly not to send them out of the country" (5:9-10).

The church understands that the government wants control over the lives of the people of faith. The test comes in the form of a coin (12:17). Is God truly sovereign? "Yes," says the Markan church. "You can render to the government what belongs to the government, but your life belongs to God—even if it means you must lose your life because of Caesar. It will be okay because ultimately you belong to God."

"Take up your cross and follow me," says Jesus to the disciples and to the Markan church. For this suffering congregation, death has been redefined through Jesus' portrait of power and pain. The cross becomes not a symbol of defeat and shame, but rather the way to liberation.

The Markan church community is in crisis. On one hand, the Jewish leadership has deteriorated into a wealthy, aristocratic collection of puppets for the house of Herod. On the other hand, the Roman government still demands that Christians claim Caesar as Lord. The community is in great pain, facing extreme persecution, no matter whether the predominant population is Gentile or Jewish. Crisis is in the air the community wants to write its story. The community wants to collect the stories of Jesus and tell them in such a way that the people can find strength to meet the demands of the day.

The Portrait of the Reader

In the art of portraiture, three portraits are formed: the one who is actually painted, the one who is doing the painting, and the one who observes the final portrait. If one is studying the portrait carefully, a self-portrait emerges. Tom Boomershine says that when our personal stories intersect with the ancient story, God's presence is revealed. Boomershine calls the intersection a "sacramental moment when ordinary human reality discloses the presence of God. Through the words of the story, the WORD of God becomes present."[4]

People all over the world read Mark's Gospel, see Jesus' portrait, and see their own faces as well. For the church in the Philippines, the Markan portrait of Jesus as suffering Christ intersects with the Filipinos' story of suffering. Benedictine sister Mary John Mananzan knows about the suffering of her people and uses Mark's portrait to bring them consolation. During Holy Week the church sings the *Pasyon*. This custom depicts Christ as a humble poor person who manages to attract a huge following from the poor and oppressed. Christ is portrayed as a leader of a popular movement that threatened Roman rule and criticized traditional Jewish leadership. For a country under submission to Spain until 1898, and now struggling to establish a healthy relationship with the United States, the suffering Jesus speaks to the emancipatory struggle of the people in the country.[5]

The Markan portrait of Christ also paints the struggle of Iranian Mehdi Dibaj, who at age fifty-nine was released from prison after being arrested for converting to Christianity from Islam. Originally serving a death sentence for his apostasy, he was finally released from prison, where he had been persecuted for more than ten years for his faith in Christ.[6]

What about your story and mine? Where do we see our faces in the portrait of Jesus in Mark? Perhaps not through religious persecution or political injustice as described above. Our story is less dramatic, but no less important. Many of us come face to face with the polarities of power and pain in Mark's portrait. We, like the disciples in Mark, are infatuated with the promise of power—a special seat in the kingdom, a chance to control the scene from the top. We really like the miracles best. We like to see Jesus heal people, draw demons from the unclean and send them into swine, put the opposition in their place by well-designed phrases and logic. We like the first seven chapters of Mark the best. They please us, make us feel good. Like Peter, we tend to deny that faith does not always look good, that sometimes doing the will of God hurts.

Nevertheless, the good/bad news of the portrait is that Jesus as power is just a part of Mark's picture. There is more, much more. If we can only see the portrait of power, we have been tricked by the optical illusion. In the reality of Jesus' life and in the life of every believer there is the great paradox of power and pain. Paul describes the paradox this way: "My . . . power is made perfect in weakness. . . . For whenever I am weak, then I am strong" (2 Cor 12:9-10). The reality of the Christian life is that faith comes to us in paradoxes, in statements that seem self-contradictory but, after reflection, are essentially true. One of the greatest paradoxes of all time is that in order to find life, you must lose it.

Parker Palmer reminds us that the paradox of the gospel can be seen even in the physical structure of the cross.[7] The intersecting pieces of wood suggest the oppositions of life—left and right, up and down. We are constantly being pulled from the horizontal to the vertical and back again. Palmer says, "To walk the way of the cross is to be impaled upon contradictions, torn by opposition and tension and conflict."[8] The cross also represents the place where the contradictions converge. In the cross, life is lived with the reality of suffering and the promise of resurrection. To see power in suffering, glory in crosses, and abundance in loss is to view Mark's portrait of Jesus. And the cross stands as a mighty monument to the paradox of our faith. Jesus died so that we might live. How strange!

Perhaps it is in embracing the pain of failure—of failing an exam, of failing at relationships, of failing to receive the job promotion—that we can see Christ. The Christian faith was never intended to be a quick, get rich, get power, get health, scheme. The Markan community carved the gospel of Christ

36

into written documents while their hands were covered with blood, their brows were knitted together in anxiety, and their hearts were pounding as they searched for hiding places. But the story of Good Friday gave them Easter hope. The portrait of a bloody cross gave them focus during their own days of persecution. They wanted to tell others to hang in there and not lose hope. The church was learning that there is power in pain, strength in weakness. Mark's portrait still hangs in the gallery so that we today might learn the paradox, lean into the contradictions, and love the cross—for Christ's sake and ours!

Notes

[1]Sharyn Dowd, *Prayer, Power, and the Problem of Suffering*, SBL Dissertation Series 105 (Atlanta: Scholars Press,1988) 134.

[2]Chad Meyers, *Binding the Strong Man: A Political Reading of Mark's Story of Jesus* (Maryknoll NY: Orbis Books, 1988) 41.

[3]Ibid., 423-47.

[4]Thomas E. Boomershine, *Story Journey: An Invitation to the Gospel as Storytelling* (Nashville: Abingdon Press, 1988) 21-22.

[5]Mary John Mananzan, "Who Is Jesus Christ? Responses from the Philippines," *In God's Image* 12.3 (1993): 39-41.

[6]Foreign Mission News Summary, Foreign Mission Board of the Southern Baptist Convention, 1-17 January, 1994.

[7]Parker Palmer, *The Promise of Paradox: A Celebration of Contradictions in the Christian Life* (Washington DC: Servant Leadership School, 1993) 37.

[8]Ibid.

For Further Reading

Meyers, Chad. *Binding the Strong Man: A Political Reading of Mark's Story of Jesus*. Maryknoll NY: Orbis Books, 1988.

Minor, Mitzi. *The Spirituality of Mark: Responding to God*. Louisville KY: Westminster/John Knox Press, 1996.

Rhoads, David and Donald Mitchie. *Mark as Story: An Introduction to the Narrative of a Gospel*. Philadelphia: Fortress Press, 1982.

Tolbert, Mary Ann. "Mark" in *The Women's Bible Commentary*. Ed. by Carol A. Newsome and Sharon H. Ringe. Louisville KY: Westminster/John Knox Press, 1992.

Chapter 2

The Portrait of Jesus
in Matthew

The Matthean community—like the congregation surrounding Mark, Luke, and John—did not abstract the person and life of Jesus into some musty, dusty history book filled with endless pages of meticulous detail. Because Jesus' life and death meant something more than simply preserving historical relics, the church wrote about its Savior in a lively narrative—a story. Jesus Christ became flesh and lived with them through their literary portrait. The church presented Jesus in ways that spoke to their own life stories of political oppression, religious isolation, cultural confusion, and racial tension. This Jesus was relevant, encased in passages of a literary document so that the struggling community of faith might have a picture to place in their wallets and etch on their hearts.

For the community surrounding Mark's Gospel, the portrait was dark, evoking tones of suffering and pain. For the community surrounding the evangelist Matthew, Jesus was painted as a teacher clothed in the garb of a Jewish rabbi. The Matthean Jesus knew the art of teaching and used teachable moments to bring the gospel of redemption to life.

The Favorite Gospel

The Gospel of Matthew has been called the Gospel of the church. We do not know why the early church in the second and third centuries elevated this Gospel above the others.

Perhaps it was because Matthew is the only Gospel to use the term "church" (16:18; 18:17). Maybe this Gospel spoke most directly to the specific needs of Jewish-Christian congregations trying to form a new understanding of faith in light of the mother tradition of Judaism.

Matthew's Gospel—tinted with the hues of the Jewish world and filled with Old Testament allusions and direct quotations—would have been fascinating reading for Jewish Christians who worshiped in synagogues, revered the Torah, and kept holy feast days. Jesus' portrait in Matthew would have been familiar, for Jesus responded to the disciples and the crowds much like a Jewish rabbi.

For whatever reason, the early church writers used Matthew's Gospel more than Mark, Luke, or John. It was the Gospel that the early church used most in teaching and worship. Commentators and preachers frequently wrote and preached from the text of Matthew. As early as 115, Ignatius, the bishop of Antioch, quoted directly from Matthew's Gospel. In the early third century, Origen (185–254) provided a full-scale commentary on the Gospel, portions of which are extant.

Early church writers were convinced that Matthew was written first and that the apostle Matthew was the author. The first authorial attribution is found in a statement of Papias— bishop of Hierapolis in Phrygia around 130—that was quoted by Eusebius in the fourth century in *Ecclesiastical History* III. 39, 16. Papias said that "Matthew collected the sayings in the Hebrew language and that each one translated [or interpreted] them as best he could." But Papias' saying is not really clear. We do not know what he meant by "sayings," or exactly the identification of the Hebrew dialect. Later, when Origen wrote his commentary on the Gospel, he understood Papias to mean that Matthew, one of Jesus' apostles, first wrote a Gospel in Hebrew and then translated it into Greek. Other writers, such as Irenaeus, Jerome, and Augustine, thought the same. In their understanding, Matthew wrote first. Mark was simply the abbreviator of Matthew's Gospel.

To accept Matthew as written prior to the writing of Mark seems difficult for two reasons. If, as Papias said, Matthew was written in the Hebrew dialect, the Gospel of Matthew gives no overt traces of having been translated even from Aramaic. No foreign syntax or loan words are evident. The Greek is well developed and superior to that of Mark. Second, to say that Matthew was written first and then copied by Mark, one must explain why Mark omitted nearly 50 percent of Matthew's Gospel—and that remains difficult to do. Matthew, although probably not the first Gospel to be written, remained the favorite of the church for many years.

The bottom line is that we do not really know for sure who wrote this Gospel, nor its original language. No signatures can be found even among the oldest Gospel manuscripts. It bears only the imprint of a community that worshiped Jesus as Teacher and Lord. We are the fortunate benefactors of their literary gifts and faithful lives. We can, therefore, read this Gospel with thanksgiving for the portrait of Christ it paints and for the lives of the painters.

Jesus' Portrait

As in the other Gospels, Matthew's portrait of Jesus has many dimensions. Jesus is preacher, teacher, and healer, but the predominant portrait is Jesus as teacher. Matthew intentionally characterizes Jesus as the Jewish rabbi, the one who has great wisdom and imparts that knowledge to others. The structure of the Gospel itself shows that catechetical concerns, instructions for missionaries, and teachings regarding discipline in the church community are foremost in the minds of the congregation. This is a teaching Gospel, and the primary portrait of Jesus is that of teacher.

The portrait of Jesus has a clear Jewish tone. Notice the opening words of Matthew's Gospel: "An account of the genealogy of Jesus the Messiah, the son of David, the son of Abraham" (1:1). No other Gospel begins with a long record of Jesus' family tree (1:1-17). Why does Matthew introduce the Gospel in this manner? Genealogical tables were important in Jewish tradition (Gen 4:7-22, 5:1-32, 10:1-32, 11:10-26; Exod 6:14-25; Num 3:1-2, 17-20; 1 Chron 1:1–9:4). Records of lineage were important for the protection of inheritances, land claims, and the preservation of the purity of blood lines. Matthew uses a Jewish genealogical list to introduce Jesus as a part of the Jewish heritage. As son of Abraham, Jesus is related to the Hebrew nation. And as the Son of David, Jesus has a right to participate in the royal heritage as well.

If you are sleeping when this family tree is read, as many readers are, you are going to miss some great surprises. Trumpet blasts disguised as whispers reside in Matthew's genealogical table. Unexpected jolts of lightning hit the first-century reader and may shock you as well. The first question asked by the ancient and modern reader is probably: "How did those women get in there?"

Look carefully at the list, and you will see Tamar (1:3), Rahab (1:5), Ruth (1:5), and the wife of Uriah (1:6). They are not your traditional, pietistic, Jewish matriarchs. You might expect to see Sarah or Rachel, maybe even a Miriam or Deborah, or perhaps an Esther in the list, but certainly not these women. Tamar disguised herself as a prostitute and seduced her father-in-law, Judah, in order to provide descendants for the nation of Israel (Gen 38). From her younger son, Perez, came Boaz, the husband of Ruth. Her assertive actions ensured an unbroken lineage in salvation history. Rahab, a Canaanite and a prostitute, marginalized by all accounts, played a major role in the history of Israel by saving the lives of Israelite spies (Josh 2–6). Ruth, a poor, widowed, foreigner from Moab, married Boaz after sleeping with him on the threshing floor and became the great-grandmother of King David (Ruth 3). Following Naomi's advice, Ruth's loyalty and cleverness secured a future for her family and for the future of Israel. Bathsheba, wife of Uriah, the Hittite, obeyed the demands of King David to be his mistress and wife and became the mother of Solomon (2 Sam 11:1-26). Mary, the last woman listed in the genealogy, became pregnant before her marriage to Joseph and gave birth to Jesus (Matt 1:18). Matthew's non-traditional genealogy, with its unusual list of Jewish and foreign women, has many twists and surprises.

How does one explain this unconventional genealogy? Some of the early church fathers suggested that these women were included as examples of sinners who needed redemption. Other interpreters wrote that the inclusion of foreign women, such as Rahab and Ruth, in the genealogy foreshadowed the inclusion of Gentiles into the church. Both interpretations remain unconnected to the central message of Matthew's Gospel. These women are not to be seen simply as unredeemed sinners nor as excluded foreigners. Rather, the women in Matthew's genealogy are exemplars of higher righteousness (Matt 5:20). Amy-Jill Levine suggests that the women are in the family tree because they exhibit the "higher righteousness" that Jesus teaches in Matthew's Sermon on the Mount.[1]

> Tamar acts when Judah unjustly refuses; Rahab recognizes the power of the Hebrew God and so protects the scouts; Uriah (who is named in the genealogy, whereas Bathsheba is not named)—unlike David—displays fidelity to his commission and his fellow soldiers; and Ruth, following Naomi's advice, moves Boaz to action.[2]

The men, Judah, the king of Jericho, David, and Boaz, who had the power to respond, fail to characterize righteousness. By contrast, those without power, The women, who have been marginalized by the tradition and weakened by societal standards, become the examples of higher righteousness in Matthew's Gospel. The women are willing to defy societal expectations in order to respond to divine purposes. Jesus, likewise, responds to life with the same boldness. These women belong to Jesus' family tree and to the community of faith.

With this genealogical table, Matthew also says to the Jewish-Christian community, "Jesus belongs." Jesus is not a foreign entity imported from some extraterrestrial country. Jesus is the son of Abraham, the son of David. Jesus is to be respected in the same way that the tradition reveres Father Abraham. Jesus is to be adored as the kingly heir of the divine Davidic family tree.

Jack Dean Kingsbury observes the close connection between Jesus and Abraham and suggests that Jesus conveys the promise unfulfilled by Abraham. Because of Jesus, God will extend to the nations the blessing of salvation (8:11; 28:19-20), as originally promised to Abraham.[3]

As son of David, Jesus fulfills prophecy, although not without a few twists and surprises. Jesus had to be adopted by Joseph, because the Davidic lineage came through Joseph's side of the family, not Mary's. In 1:16, the final link of the genealogy is broken. Instead of repeating the phrases "and Jacob fathered Joseph, and Joseph fathered Jesus," the text breaks the formulaic pattern and states: "and Jacob fathered Joseph the husband of Mary, of whom Jesus was born" (1:16). Jesus had to be adopted. Because of the faithfulness of Joseph, Jesus becomes the legitimate son of David.

The Son of David theme continues throughout the Gospel. As the Son of David, Jesus enters Jerusalem and takes possession, not as a warrior but as the prince of peace. Likewise, Jesus performs acts of healing as the Son of David (15:21-28; 21:15). Because the people confess that Jesus is Israel's Davidic messiah, the people find blessing. The portraits of Jesus as son of Abraham and son of David are important to the Gospel of Matthew. Another picture, however, looms even larger, using more canvas and narrative space than the stories of Abraham and David. Jesus is the Jewish teacher.

Jesus, the Teacher

Rest your eyes for a few moments from the other pictures of Jesus in Matthew and concentrate on this particularly strong portrait—Jesus as teacher. Often this one has been overlooked by theologians looking for christological titles to identify Jesus. Matthean scholars have chosen to focus on more lofty words, such as Son of God or Messiah, to describe Jesus in Matthew's Gospel. That Jesus is a teacher, however, cannot be denied in this Gospel. Jesus' own words acknowledge the title. Furthermore, the very structure of the narrative with its five major discourses, or "teachable moments," underscore Jesus' role as teacher and the listeners as obedient learners. As we view the church's gallery of portraits of Jesus, Matthew's picture of Jesus as teacher can neither be overlooked nor minimized.

First, Jesus' own words in the narrative identify this teaching role: "A disciple is not above the teacher" (10:24); "But you are not to be called rabbi, for you have one teacher" (23:8); "Say to him, 'The Teacher says, My time is near' " (26:18). Although the disciples never call Jesus "teacher," Jewish scribes, Pharisees, Sadducees, lawyers, tax collectors, and a wealthy young man acknowledge Jesus' teaching function (8:19; 9:11; 12:38; 17:24; 19:16; 22:16, 24, 36). In Matthew's Gospel, Jesus reveals God's will by teaching basic instructions for daily living. Because of Jesus' public teaching and its radical content, Jesus is killed in Matthew.

Second, the very structure of the Gospel supports Jesus' role as teacher. The Gospel contains five great didactic units, sometimes called the discourses or speeches of Jesus: 5:1–7:29; 10:5–11:1; 13:1–53a; 18:1–19:1a; 24:1–26:1a. I choose to call them Matthew's "teachable moments." Teachable moments are those times, often unrehearsed and unplanned, when the opportunity for teaching and learning matches the needs of the learner. We all learn better when we know that we need the material. For example, the seminary student who knows that weekly sermon preparation will be an important role in one's future job as pastor gives special attention to the preaching course. Successful learning occurs when the teaching material matches the needs of the learner.

It was the same for the characters of the Matthew's narrative world and for the community that shaped the narrative. Jesus teaches at that particular moment when the disciples and the crowds are most receptive to his words. Some forty years later, Matthew's church community hear these same teachable moments from Jesus at the time when they are most eager to learn.

These teachable moments punctuate the Gospel at strategic points. The five great speeches are presented after the infancy narrative and before the story of Jesus' death and resurrection. Coupled with each speech is an introductory narrative. These five teachable moments further underscore Jesus' role as teacher, as well as the Matthean community's need to hear the teaching of Jesus within their own first-century world.

Teachings on Righteousness
The Sermon on the Mount (5:1–7:29)

Introducing this teaching unit, traditionally called the Sermon on the Mount, is a narrative (3:1–4:25) that highlights Jesus' teaching theme. In conversation with John the Baptist Jesus announces: "for it is proper for us in this way to fulfill all righteousness" (3:15). The fulfillment of the theme of righteousness is then graphically illustrated in the first teaching unit—the Sermon on the Mount.

Identify the listeners in 4:24. These great crowds are not the normal pretty people of society. They are the sick, those with various diseases and pains, the demoniacs, epileptics, and paralytics. They are searching for healing. The disciples are also there. They appear to be the closest to Jesus, although the crowds are probably not far away and can still hear Jesus' voice. Jesus has offered healing to the sick and has called some new disciples. Now in this great teachable moment, when the sick have crawled and stumbled hoping to be healed and when some raw, earthy fishermen sit anxiously waiting for an orientation lesson to their new life, Jesus teaches.

He sits down (5:1) in typical Jewish rabbinic fashion, and they listen. Using familiar Old Testament sounds of blessing, Jesus vividly describes the reign of God with these beatitudes: "Blessed are the poor in spirit, for theirs is the kingdom of heaven. Blessed are those who mourn, for they will be comforted." This picture is intended to teach what it means to live in the midst of God's rule.

Attributes such as mourning, meekness, spiritual hunger and thirst, forgiveness, purity of heart, and peacemaking are not signs of weakness in the life of faith, but rather signs of power. To a group of people with heavy backs burdened by physical pain and spiritual confusion and to a new crew of green disciples, Jesus speaks important truths to live by. These folk have been broken by the injustices of society and the reality of physical pain. They listen carefully, for they are hungry to be taught. It is a teachable moment.

The lesson plan is not over; there is more to come. In 5:21-48, Jesus teaches with a radicality unparalleled in Jewish religious life: "You have heard that it was said . . . but I say to you." Jesus boldly rebukes the surface nature of the Law and brings the reality of faith right into the center of the heart when he says it is not enough simply not to murder. If you have unresolved anger in your heart, you have already started the process of killing your neighbor. Likewise, it is not enough simply to refrain from adultery. If you have thought about it in your heart, you have committed the sin. The rhetorical force of these antithetical statements shocks the hearers. Predictably for the listening members of the religious establishment, Jesus' radical teaching encourages visions of how this revolutionary mouth must be muffled.

As Jesus teaches, those who listen carefully hear the main point—"unless your righteousness exceeds that of the scribes and Pharisees" (5:20). Through the clear teaching of Jesus, the crowds get the picture that Jesus is introducing a *new* community of faith.

Teachings on Travel
The Missionary Speech (10:5–11:1)

In 8–10:4 the community of Matthew's Gospel creates an introduction to the second great teachable moment in this Gospel. The introductory unit educates the reader in the many responsibilities of discipleship. In this introductory section, Jesus performs a cascade of miracles. He calms a stormy sea and heals a paralytic, a ruler's daughter, a bleeding woman, two blind men, and one mute. Then he turns to the disciples and says, "Go and do likewise."

The text does not give us the disciples' verbal response at this point. But if that had been me, after having seen all that

47

Jesus had accomplished prior to my commissioning, I would have wanted to say, "Whoa, wait a minute here. Sorry, but the job description is too broad. I cannot see myself effectively meeting all those goals and objectives."

Maybe my response is not that different from that of the disciples, for after Jesus appoints them for the mission, he then has to teach them and carefully prepare them for their future. They listen carefully, for they have been given the mandate, but they do not yet know how to do it. It is another teachable moment. It is during the moments of intense panic—when the computer has a glitch, or the refrigerator has broken down again, or when you are being sent to places you do not want to go to do things you think you are not capable of doing—that it always helps to have a handbook or a list of detailed instructions. In this teachable moment (10:5–11:1), Jesus gives a detailed manual to the disciples that includes what to wear on one's back, what to carry in one's purse, and what to do even when you are rejected. Jesus teaches, and the disciples listen, for their very lives depend on it.

The specifics are important here. The faces of the disciples show that they are about to panic. No abstract, philosophical summary of journeying will do. A specific, step-by-step presentation is essential. Otherwise, how will they begin to fulfill this enormous job description?

Obviously, it is important to know where to go and where not to go. Jesus teaches the disciples that they are to go to the Jews. "Don't go to the Gentiles or Samaritans. That will come later. Go to your own homefolk first—your aunts, uncles, cousins, family, and friends." Then Jesus teaches them what to say and do: proclaim that God has arrived, and take care of the people's needs (10:7-8).

Perhaps the disciples are thinking by now, "What about the honorarium?" And Jesus replies, "There is none, other than for your basic needs. So, take no money with you, nor suitcase, sandals, or staff, not even a second coat. For your needs will be taken care of by others along the journey." Hospitality will be provided in people's homes.

These practical suggestions are given. You can imagine the disciples feverishly taking notes from the teacher's presentation. They are perhaps thinking, "No problem now; we can handle this. This might even be fun—meeting new people, preaching a little, and healing folk."

But then you can hear their gasp of disbelief and maybe even the first moment of regret, regret that they have decided to follow their teacher. Jesus is beginning to teach that there will be those who will not like them, that some people will not want to receive them nor even listen to them, and that some people will want to beat them and drag them before councils and synagogues for trials and punishments.

The disciples swallow hard, take a big gulp of air, and try to process all that they are hearing. They say, "Rejection? We never thought that it would be like this. Where can we sign out of this course? Anybody got any withdrawal slips?"

Jesus does provide a way out, although not from the actual persecution but from the bitterness and internalized anger that rejection often creates. Jesus gives the disciples a ritual that will symbolically release their anger, soften their bitterness, and give them strength for ministry in the next town. Jesus says, "If anyone will not welcome you or listen to your words, shake off the dust from your feet as you leave that house or town" (10:14). Jesus gives explicit instructions for living with persecution in the remaining verses of chapter 10. The tone is serious, but the words also give assurance that God is in control even when the outer circumstances look bleak. Surely the God who has numbered the hairs of the disciples' heads will care for them and offer them protection for their journey. The second teaching unit concludes in 11:1: "Now when Jesus had finished instructing his twelve disciples, he went on from there to teach and proclaim his message in their cities."

Teachings on the Secrets of the Kingdom
The Parables Discourse (13:1-53)

Jesus continues teaching. An interlude occurs between the two didactic units of the missionary and parable discourses. Verses 2-12 in chapter 11 serve as an introductory section for Jesus' third teaching unit, the parables. This introductory section prepares the way for the parable instruction. The crowds are introduced in 11:7-24. The people who followed Jesus looking for miracles still do not understand the mysteries of the kingdom. Jesus rebukes them for the negative critique of his friend and forerunner, John the Baptist (11:2-19). Notice that Jesus' language appears more emphatic than we have seen before in the Gospel. Jesus chides them for not accepting John. He came fasting, and the people thought he had a demon (11:18). Furthermore, Jesus came eating and drinking, and the crowds thought he was a glutton and a drunkard. Can these people not see reality?

The language becomes even more violent as Jesus responds to those who have seen miracles but whose lives have gone unchanged: "On the day of judgment it will be more tolerable for Tyre and Sidon than for you [Chorazin and Bethsaida]"(11:22). Even Capernaum, the base of Jesus' mission and adult hometown, does not go without judgment (11:23-24).

The kingdom looks different from what the crowds expect. Jesus sets out to show them. In the new life with God, if one is hungry, it is acceptable to pluck grain on the Sabbath. Something greater than the Jewish tradition or temple has arrived on the scene, namely Jesus the Teacher (12:5), who is also Lord of the Sabbath (12:8). In this new life with God, if one sees a person in need, like a man with a withered hand outside the synagogue, then that man can be healed—even if it is the Sabbath (12:9-14).

Jesus provides enough irritation so that the Pharisees begin to devise a plan to destroy him (12:14), but not before they try to figure him out. They ask one more time for clarification:

"Teacher, we wish to see a sign from you" (12:38). Jesus invokes the story of Jonah, admonishing those who hear to repent as the city of Ninevah did after hearing Jonah's preaching. Because something greater than Jonah is here, the people should likewise repent. But no response.

The strong, violent language of Jesus prompts the listeners to want to know more about this new life with God. What does it look like? How can one live a fruitful life (12:33-36)? How can one escape judgment (12:42)?

Jesus begins to teach in parables in the third great teachable moment in Matthew. The listeners are ready. In the first half of the chapter Jesus teaches from a boat (13:1-35). In the second part of the chapter Jesus teaches in a house (13:36-52). Two teaching locales and two different responses to Jesus' teaching emerge from this didactic moment. In the boat, the crowds listen to the parables and do not understand. In the house, the disciples listen to parables and understand, unlike the disciples in Mark.

The teachings of Jesus in the boat use common agricultural metaphors of seeds and weeds. The seeds have been planted; some fall on good soil, and others on poor soil. Those that fall on good soil produce a great harvest. Those that fall on poor soil wither and blow away. To the crowds, Jesus says, "The one who has ears, let that one hear." But they don't.

Again Jesus teaches. The kingdom of heaven is like a man who planted good wheat seed in his field (13:24-30), but an enemy came during the night and planted weeds among the wheat. The servants are anxious to rid the soil of the bad seed. The owner, however, cautions them against hasty actions that may endanger the good crop. He advises them to wait until harvest when the wheat and the tares can be separated without hurting the wheat. The crowds make no response.

Again Jesus teaches. The kingdom of heaven is like a mustard seed . . . the kingdom of heaven is like leaven hidden in flour. The crowds are still silent. They are prepared to learn. Jesus has made it clear in the introductory section that kingdom living is going to be different. His language has cautioned them to be alert and to learn a new way of living with God.

Although from the teacher's perspective this didactic moment is appropriate, the crowds make no response.

Compare the response of the crowds with that of the disciples in the house (13:36-52). Jesus teaches the disciples that the kingdom of heaven is like treasure hidden in a field . . . like a merchant in search of fine pearls . . . like a net thrown into the sea (13:44-50). As Jesus concludes his teaching unit, he asks the disciples, "Have you understood all this?" (13:51). And they reply simply, "Yes." Unlike the disciples in Mark, the disciples in Matthew seem to understand what Jesus is saying. In Matthew, Jesus teaches, and the disciples respond.

Teachings on the Church
The Ecclesial Discourse (18:1–19:1)

Chapters 14–17 provide the introduction to the teaching material on the church. In this fourth teachable moment in Matthew's Gospel, Jesus the teacher describes the church. The listeners are prepared to hear.

The theme of the introductory unit is the church. Stories about Simon Peter, a leader in the early church, are told. After Simon Peter has tried to walk on water (14:28-31), he confesses that Christ is the Son of the Living God (16:18). And upon that confession, Jesus builds his church (*ekklesia*). Simon receives a new name and becomes known as the "rock" (*petros*). The church is built on the confession of Peter, not on Peter's merit or ability to understand all the implications of faith. This one is the same man who later would have to be censured for misunderstanding Jesus' destiny (16:21-23). Peter is also the babbling mouth making inappropriate speeches in the awesome, holy moment of Jesus' transfiguration (17:1-13). The church, not built on the perfections or imperfections of its apostolic forebears, resides in the confessions of those who call Jesus Christ the Son of God.

In the same section two feeding stories are seen. One miraculous display of food is for the five thousand (14:13-21) and the other for the four thousand (15:32-39). One is for the

Jew and the other for the Gentile. Together, and only together, these two parts make up one whole body called the church. The new Israel is one, purified, reshaped, and made new in these stories.

The listeners are ready. It is a teachable moment again. Something new is in the air. The parts are beginning to fit together—Peter's confession, the multiple feeding stories on both sides of the sea, the new Israel. But what does the church look like? What does it mean to live in the new community of faith?

In the fourth teachable moment, Jesus gives clear answers to questions about the church. It is different, that is for sure. In the new community, Jesus says, the leaders look like children (18:1-8); however, not in the way they throw their peas as toddlers or refuse to do their homework as adolescents. The church is made up of people who realize that just as children depend on parental support for their needs, so must the people of God depend on God.

Jesus teaches that some of the fold will be tempted to sin, and the community must try to protect them. Just as the shepherd goes after the one lost sheep, so must the church find the "little ones" (18:6-14). Furthermore, if members are not always in harmony, there are guidelines given for restoration. Relationships are extremely important to the church (18:15-21). Finally, Jesus declares that forgiveness is the primary activity of the church (18:21-34). Jesus teaches, and the disciples listen.

Teachings on the End of Time
The Eschatological Discourse (24:1–26:1)

The disciples are ready to hear the eschatological teachings of Jesus. They have been prepared to hear a lesson on what to expect as the end draws near. They have been with Jesus, and the tension has increased in the last few hours. In the introduction to this discourse (chaps. 19–23), Jesus has entered Jerusalem, cursed a fig tree, cleansed the temple by driving out the merchants, denounced the scribes and Pharisees in a long series of woes, and cried over the lost city of Jerusalem. Something is about to happen. The disciples know it. Now Jesus has their full attention as they sit on the Mount of Olives reflecting on all that they have seen and heard in the last few hours.

Jesus begins to teach them about the end of time. The lesson is not fun to hear. It causes them great concern to hear Jesus speak this way. They remain quiet as Jesus tells them of the coming suffering, the great tribulation, and the coming of the Son of Man (24:1-32). The hardest part to hear is that Jesus will not tell when the end of time will occur. No one knows. Jesus teaches that they should simply be prepared for whenever it may happen. The message of Jesus' teachings here is to be ready regardless of the hour (24:36-51).

Jesus cannot cease teaching. Using parables, Jesus teaches the disciples how to prepare for the end. While waiting for the end of time, the disciples are to stay prepared, like the five faithful maidens who had extra oil for their lamps (25:1-13). Disciples are to be wise stewards, like the one who invested five talents (vv. 14-30). Jesus says that it is not enough to wait passively for the end of time. While waiting, faithful disciples will also feed the hungry, clothe the naked, and care for the sick (vv. 31-46).

Jesus' words become actions in the closing chapters of Matthew's Gospel. His own death is imminent. He has taught that disciples are to be actively involved in the life of faith. Now Jesus himself sets the example with his actions as he waits to die. He does not passively wait to die but uses each moment to prepare the disciples for his farewell.

He plans to share a final meal with his disciples. He asks them to enter Jerusalem, find a certain individual, and say, "The Teacher says, My time is near" (26:18). The Teacher spends time with his disciples, sharing a meal with them that the church will continue to remember for centuries. The Teacher desires that his students be close to him while he prays in the garden, but they fall asleep (vv. 36-46). Jesus

THE PORTRAIT OF JESUS IN MATTHEW

prepares to die. The voice of the Teacher is finally silent. The lessons are over. The words are heard no more.

On the third day, however, Mary Magadelene and other women go to the tomb and discover that Jesus Christ, their Teacher, has risen. Jesus' instructions are not over. Jesus, the Teacher, has more to say, even after the resurrection. The women are instructed to tell the disciples to go to Galilee and wait for Jesus there.

The disciples go to Galilee and wait. And as Jesus has promised, he appears. He has one more lesson to teach. Jesus the Teacher gives one final word of instruction to his disciples that the Matthean congregation continues to hear ringing in their ears: "As you are going, make disciples of all the nations, baptizing them in the name of the Father and of the Son and of the Holy Spirit, teaching them to observe all that I have commanded you. And remember I am with you always, even until the end of the age" (28:19-20).

The Portrait of the Community

What kind of people contributed to Jesus' portrait as teacher in Matthew's Gospel? Who were they? When were they working together? Where did they live?

The precise dating of the writing of the Gospel of Matthew is impossible to determine. We can only make conjectures. From the text itself we can surmise that the writing took place after the fall of Jerusalem in 70. The parable of the Great Supper suggests an awareness of the destruction of Jerusalem (23:1-14). Members of the community were probably Jewish Christians, although the group could have included Gentiles who understood the symbols from the Jewish tradition. The community was at home perhaps in Antioch of Syria.

The lack of concrete information regarding date, place, and composition of community can be frustrating. We want to be able to locate the Gospel in its chronological framework, but we have no strong external or internal pieces of evidence. The text, however, provides for another way of viewing the community. Although we cannot infer much historical data, we can view the Gospel of Matthew as a piece of communication that would reveal the community's world. Remember that a portrait has the potential to reveal three faces: the subject, the artist, and the one viewing the piece of work. Based on that premise we can explore the portrait of Jesus in Matthew and discover the faces of the community.

Our questions are different, however. The historical need to date the document fades, and our interests are personal—more sociological—in nature. We can read the text and ask these questions: What was the community's greatest theological and social concern? Who were their opponents? What were they trying to say about themselves as they told their story of Jesus? What was the social texture of their life?

Obviously, the community was at home with teaching and teachers. Krister Stendahl, in his 1954 dissertation, attributed the Gospel of Matthew to a group of Christian scribes who wished to provide a handbook for the early Christian community.[4] Although Stendahl's work never reached majority opinion among New Testament Matthean scholars, his dissertation did generate new ideas about communities and schools behind the Gospels. Whether or not the Gospel of Matthew was actually produced by a group of scribes or if the Gospel was truly a handbook for the early church community, we may never know with certitude. Stendahl's thesis, however, clearly points us to the unique didactic character of this Gospel.

Intentional attempts are made to provide learning experiences in this Gospel. While the material may also have been used by the church for liturgical and homiletical purposes, the Gospel also bears the mark of a catechetical document. The community's stylized portrait of Jesus as a learned, Jewish rabbi featured in five, clearly-structured, didactic sections in the Gospel narrative attests to their own desire to teach and to learn. This Matthean community of faith huddled around the Gospel because it provided training for their particular challenges of life.

The community experienced intense conflict from two sides—the Gentile authorities and the Jewish religious tradition. Consequently, for them, education was the best response they could give to such a hostile situation. These Jewish Christians were living in close proximity to hostile pagans. Hauled into court by Gentile authorities, harassed, hated by everyone, and eventually executed, the members of the Matthean church were shaping a Gospel that taught new members how to live under such extreme conditions (10:18, 22; 13:21; 24:9).

On the other side, adding to their social trauma, were the pressures from the Jewish community. The Matthean community was probably living close to an energetic Jewish community. The parable of the tares implies that the church and Israel should grow up side by side until the harvest (13:24-30). The presence of the story of the temple tax provides another example of the pressure the community felt from their Jewish neighbors. They felt the demand to contribute to the Jewish collection for Jamnia.

In the meantime, how did they live? On one side, they observed the freedom from the law of the Gentiles. They saw no boundaries of morality and values. On the other side, they observed the strict codes of law and tight boundaries of behavior from the Jewish perspective. How did they understand what it really meant to be a follower of Christ?

Carl Dudley and Earle Hilgert, authors of *New Testament Tensions and the Contemporary Church*, describe the energy of the Matthean community as the "urgency of faithfulness."[5] The church had not been driven to despair but to faithfulness. Confused over Gentile and Jewish relationships, and all the while unsure as to when Jesus' return would be, the community could have disintegrated. Instead, the state of confusion became productive for the Matthean community.

The time of confusion became a period of great growth for the community of Matthew's Gospel. In this search for a faithful response in the midst of pressures from both sides, they heard their teacher's voice ring clearly from the mountain: "For I tell you, unless your righteousness exceeds that of the scribes and Pharisees, you will never enter the kingdom of heaven" (5:20). They continued to listen, and Jesus kept teaching: "You have heard that . . . you shall not murder, . . . but I say to you that if you are angry . . ." (5:21-22). And because of Jesus' teachings, the Matthean community learned how to live in the midst of religious legalism and undisciplined freedom.

The Portrait of the Reader

What do we look like in this Gospel? We look like we have often tried to ignore it. For some reading Jesus' radical teachings, it is easier just to admit that the teachings are not relevant for the masses. Some readers conclude that the teachings of Jesus are really just intended for an inner, select group of followers, for the super righteous, like those who take monastic vows, never raise their voices, eat daily from the four food groups, and constantly pray and smile. After all, everyone knows that those who have to fight rush-hour traffic, pay electric bills, and stay home with kids who have the chicken pox are exempt from the rigors of Jesus' teachings.

Wrong! We would like to be able to say that our own portraits do not belong in this Gospel. The teachings are too hard and, thus, irrelevant for us. But we cannot get off the hook so easily.

Some of you reading this may belong in the age group born between 1961 and 1981.[6] You are an unusual group of folk. Called the thirteenth generation by some writers, generation X by others, you are currently being studied by many groups. Many people want to know what kinds of CDs you buy, what kind of cereal you eat, and what computer games you like best. You are interesting because you are caught in one, big, societal squeeze. The big spenders, including your parents, are in front of you, and they have spent all your money. Your children may end up in poverty, and you are caught somewhere in the middle. You are the first generation that does not have the promise of doing better economically than your parents.

Your folks have not only spent all of your money, but they have also left you with homes that are shattered by divorce and riveted by cultural changes in the family structure. You are labeled the "bad" generation, for you carry handguns to school and speak in abbreviated language symbols consisting mainly of inflection and gesture, called "McLanguage."

The cartoon says it best. The young college student is getting ready for morning classes. On the bed are two T-shirts. One says in bold, dark print, "JUST DO IT" and the other says, "JUST SAY NO." The caption reads, "Some days it just takes hours to get dressed."

You are in the middle, caught in the big squeeze. On one side lies unlimited freedom—freedom from relationships, service, responsibility. On the other side, you are faced with the possibility of the strict Victorianism belonging to another century. How will you live?

Watch Matthew's community—your community. The struggles of that community parallel yours. Observe Matthew's portrait of Jesus—your portrait—for Jesus has something to say to you as he did to that community 1900 years ago. To hear Jesus teach the radical demands of discipleship means to consider change. To hear the ancient words echo down from the mountain through the years of many generations is to realize that there are some values that cannot be carved from the Woodstock of the 1960s or from the Washington of the 1990s. These values are there, not to be listened to in trivial fashion, not to be considered as some nice, academic exercise, but to be lived as the Master Teacher taught them. It is a teachable moment. Hear them again:

•Do not lay up treasures for yourselves; they will rust and rot.
•No one can serve two masters; God and the world.
•Judge not lest you be judged.
•Do not be anxious about tomorrow.
•Enter by the narrow gate.
•Beware of false prophets.

Dietrich Bonhoeffer knew the costly price of doing the right and just thing. The teaching Jesus was the portrait that guided Bonhoeffer through the long days of prison and suffering in Nazi Germany. In all of that confusion, he looked to the Sermon on the Mount as a directive for his life and as a guideline for the community he served. Bonhoeffer says that to deal with the teachings of Jesus otherwise than by doing them is to wrong Jesus. Not responding actively to the teachings of Jesus in Matthew is saying no to God. Bonhoeffer said,

> Humanly speaking we could understand and interpret Jesus' teachings in a thousand different ways. Jesus knows only one possibility: simple surrender and obedience, not interpreting it but doing it.[7]

And here we are. We cannot linger in the portrait gallery analyzing Matthew's fine portrait any longer, for there is work to do. Following Jesus is not easy, but the Teacher shows us how. Thanks be to God!

Notes

[1]Amy-Jill Levine, "Matthew," *Women's Bible Commentary*, Carol A. Newsome and Sharon H. Ringe, eds. (Louisville KY: Westminster/John Knox Press, 1992) 253-54.

[2]Ibid.

[3]Jack Dean Kingsbury, *Matthew as Story* (Philadelphia: Fortress Press, 1986) 45.

[4]Krister Stendahl, *The School of St. Matthew* (Philadelphia: Fortress Press, 1969) [first published as *Acta Seminarii Neo-testamentici Upsaliensis* (Lund: C. W. K. Gleerup, 1954)] 35.

[5]Carl S. Dudley and Earle Hilgert, *New Testament Tensions and the Contemporary Church* (Philadelphia: Fortress Press, 1987) 88-90.

[6]Neil Howe and Bill Strauss, *13th Generation: Abort, Retry, Ignore, Fail?* (New York: Random House, 1993).

[7]Dietrich Bonhoeffer, *The Cost of Discipleship*, trans. R. H. Fuller (London: SCM Press, 1959) 175.

For Further Reading

Anderson, Janice Capel. "Matthew: Gender and Reading." *Semeia* 28 (1983): 3-27.

Deutsch, Celia M. *Lady Wisdon, Jesus and Social Context in Matthew's Gospel*. Valley Forge PA: Trinity Press International, 1996.

Edwards, Richard A. *Matthew's Story of Jesus*. Philadelphia: Fortress Press, 1985.

Fox, Emmet. *The Sermon on the Mount: The Key to Success in Life*. San Francisco: Harper, 1989. (First published in 1934 by Emmet Fox).

Meyer, Ben F. *Five Speeches that Changed the World*. Collegeville MN: Liturgical Press, 1994.

Chapter 3

The Portrait of Jesus in Luke

"To produce fine art is to push the edges of what is inexpressible into some kind of expressible form," says artist Ephraim Rubenstein. Luke's portrait of Jesus appears unconventional, pushing the edges of classical Gospel portraiture established by Mark and Matthew. Luke overlooks Matthew's traditional portrait of Jesus teaching from a mountain. Likewise, Luke gives the Markan suffering Messiah only slight attention. Luke's painting, pushing the edges of convention, situates Jesus around a common table filled with food. At this table, Jesus breaks with religious convention and eats and drinks with tax collectors, prostitutes, and sinners. With vivid detail Luke captures the extraordinary Jesus in an ordinary setting—the inexpressible becomes expressible as Jesus fellowships with friends, eating and drinking around a table.

To paint Luke's picture on canvas, you would have to add the important, although often overlooked, small details. Luke's picture of Jesus would not have special lighting to cast a mystical glow or artist-imposed halos around the central figures. Rather, the picture would be earthy, just as common as your own kitchen table on a Saturday night with friends, board games, and pizza. In the hands of Luke's first-century table guests would be goblets of wine and loaves of bread, common fare for the ancient world that would not be made uncommon until Jesus' final meal. Hands would be raised in the air to gesture a hearty laugh. Someone would have an arm thrown around another's shoulders in a warm embrace. A few guests would be locked in intense conversation. Postures would be relaxed, and the general mood would be congenial and friendly.

Luke wants us to know that this inexpressible Jesus can be expressed by pushing the traditional edges of portraiture. No stiff poses here, where postures are picture perfect and smiles are held only for a moment. No, in Luke we see that Jesus genuinely cares about people, even the not-so-pretty people of society. The mood is relaxed, unconcerned about social and religious propriety, familiar, congenial, and accepting. Luke's portrait shouts that the gospel of Christ is for everyone, not just for a few selected righteous ones. That announcement is not dogmatized by creed or ritual in Luke's Gospel. Rather, it is simply expressed by the very ordinary picture of Jesus sitting at the table with others and sharing one of life's most intimate, extraordinary moments—a meal.

An Orderly Gospel

Luke's portrait of Jesus pushes the edges and presents a literary portrait with uncommon attention to common detail. Luke is careful to place events within historical and religious time. We are told that Zechariah, the priest, served the temple "in the days of King Herod of Judea" (1:5). We also learn that John the Baptist preached "in the fifteenth year of the reign of Emperor Tiberius, when Pontius Pilate was governor of Judea, and Herod was ruler of Galilee, and his brother Philip ruler of the region of Ituraea and Trachonitis, and Lysanius ruler of Abilene, during the high priesthood of Annas and Caiaphas" (3:1). Historical details are important to the community of Luke's Gospel.

Pushing the edges in Luke also means producing a Gospel with an intentional literary structure, especially in terms of gender relationships. Male and female characters are juxtaposed in the narrative. Although women are most often cast in supportive roles to men (perhaps revealing more about the community of Luke's Gospel than the roles of women around Jesus), stories about women receive careful attention in the Gospel of Luke. For example, an angel first appears to Zechariah, then to Mary (1:11-20/1:26-38). Simeon prophesies, but then so does Anna (2:25-35/2:36-38). Jesus heals a man with an unclean spirit, then heals Simon's mother-in-law (4:31-37/4:38-39). Jesus tells a parable about a woman who loses her coins, then tells about a father who loses his son (15:8-10/15:11-24).

The prologue announces Luke's care for precision (1:1-4). Luke intends to write a Gospel that is orderly and intentional. Luke's unique purpose is seen in comparison with the beginnings of the other Gospel narratives. No other Gospel begins like Luke's. For example, the Gospel of Mark jumps into the story with little introduction announcing that Jesus Christ is the Son of God (Mark 1:1). Matthew introduces the narrative with an extended genealogical table, with parallels to Old Testament models (Matt 1:1-18). John prefaces the Gospel with a hymnic composition, full of melody and emotion.

Luke's prologue reveals a formal, Greco-Roman literary structure. C. H. Talbert compares Luke's prologue with prefaces of ancient documents from the Greco-Roman world and discovers striking similarities.[1] Similar to prefaces found in Hellenistic literature, Luke's prologue: makes a statement about predecessors; introduces the subject matter; sets forth writing credentials; announces the arrangement of the work; comments on the purpose of the writing; and names an official addressee, Theophilus.

Only one difference is found between Luke's preface and first-century introductions. While other prefaces clearly state the name of the author, Luke's prologue remains anonymous. No authorial signature exists. As with the other two Gospels, we do not know with certitude the identity of the author of this Gospel. Early tradition maintained that Luke, the physician and companion of Paul, wrote the Gospel of Luke. Although the early tradition provided a simple solution to the complex problem of authorship, certain unanswered questions challenge its assumptions. While that simplifies the task by acknowledging that Paul's friend and traveling companion wrote the book, the answer contains some mysteries. If, for example, Luke, Paul's friend and colleague in ministry, did write the Gospel and Acts, then why does the book of Acts not mention Paul's letters, his theology, or the main themes of his preaching mission? Surely if contact had been established, Paul's influence would have been seen in Luke's Gospel in some form. Furthermore, who is Luke? We have scarce information about Luke as a physician, missionary colleague, or author. Until we can find direct evidence to the contrary, we assume that the Gospel of Luke was anonymously written.

Although we may not know the author's name, we can provide a limited description of the author as revealed in the prologue. We know that the writer was not an eyewitness to the life of Jesus—for the writing of the Gospel the author depended on the memories of others (1:2). But we do know that the author was a well-educated person who knew both Old Testament traditions as well as Hellenistic literary techniques. The Gospel is written in a literary style that is more related to the vocabulary and syntax of fine literature than to everyday conversation. We know that the writer of Luke's Gospel is interested in telling the story of Jesus in Gospel narrative and wants to communicate the history of the early church, as is evident in the author's second volume, the book of Acts.

The Portrait of Jesus

The special attention Luke gives to Jesus' portrait can be compared to the care given in planning a loved one's funeral service. Eulogies of loved ones are not taken lightly. My grandmother died a few years ago, after being confined to a bed in a rest home for thirteen years, unable to speak and often not even able to recognize members of her family. At her death, we carefully planned her funeral. We wanted her to be remembered as she had lived prior to those last thirteen difficult years. I volunteered to participate in her funeral service.

I took great care as I prepared the words for her eulogy. I listened to friends and family describe her, then found a quiet place where I could remember the flood of memories from my childhood. The best descriptions of her life centered not around her literary discoveries, for she was not a woman of letters. Neither had she made important scientific experiments for the world to remember. The places of my memory centered around her common places—her garden and her kitchen—and around common events—such as meals around her table. Her table was a common place that could be remembered with all five senses. I could taste the sweetness of her corn and remember the tea perspiring on the green goblets in the heat of a summer day. I could see her best tablecloth on the kitchen table providing a hazy blue background for her treasured pieces of Blue Willow. But best of all, I could see how we all lingered around her table, eating more than we should, laughing about the events of the year, asking about the neighbors and the rest of the kinfolk, remembering past family events. At her funeral I wanted those stories told. I wanted Nanny to be remembered around her table and in her kitchen—the center of physical nourishment and family love.

Maybe this was the same kind of intensity that the community used to remember Jesus in Luke's Gospel. Persons of Luke's community remembered Jesus in a kind of unconventional way, but in a manner that was close to their heart. So they took great care when they painted their portrait. The Lukan portrait shares several basic features with the other three Gospels: Jesus' birth, his miraculous power over sickness and nature, his opposition from religious opponents, and finally, his death and resurrection. Nevertheless, common details such as food, tables, and dining room hospitality are also provided in Luke's account. Luke has pushed the edges of what is inexpressible into an expressible form and created beautiful, life-transforming art.

The literary portrait makes a distinct visual representation that creates pictorial images even for the unartistic person. If I had the ability to paint with brush and paint, I would want to draw a huge table in the center of a room. The table would be overflowing with food and drink. The dishes would be running over with food, steam reaching toward the ceiling. Jesus would be reclining, as was the first-century dining custom, beside the unacceptable people of society—the tax collectors, the sinners, the unclean. Laughter and smiles would be abundant. The table would be central in the picture because eating in Luke's Gospel reveals the heart of the gospel in a way that cannot be captured by dogma and church doctrine. Luke wants us to know that God considered sharing a meal with sinners to be at the center of the mission and ministry of Jesus Christ.

Lukan scholar Robert J. Karris also sees the dining room as the central element in Luke's portrait of Jesus. Karris observes that "in Luke's Gospel Jesus got himself crucified by the way that he ate."[2] In this particular Gospel, Jesus is constantly either going to a meal, at a meal, or coming from a meal. Place Jesus at a dining room table filled with all kinds of folk whom the religious tradition had rejected, and you will see Luke's portrait of Jesus clear and undiluted.

Jesus at Table

The theme, "The Son of man has come eating and drinking" (7:34), permeates the Gospel. Luke carefully manages the motif of food and table in the narrative like a conductor directing melodic themes in a symphony. The soft tones of the table motif are introduced in the first movement of the Gospel (1–5), where Jesus serves as the host of the table. The quiet, barely recognizable strains are bolder in the second movement when Jesus becomes the guest at the tables of others (5–20). Full melodic patterns are heard in the final movement (21–23), which brings the food motif to full denouement. The host serves the last meal, then gives his own life for the sake of others. A coda (24) then reintroduces the theme, concluding the composition by using food as a testimony to Jesus' resurrection. Jesus, the host and guest, eats and then blesses his followers and giving them hope for the future.

68

The First Movement: 1–5:9

In the first movement, the theme of food is introduced in hushed, understated tones. Luke's Gospel uses the voice of Jesus' mother, a lowly manger, and the role of master fisherman to underscore the theme of Jesus as the host of the meal.

Mary's voice introduces Jesus in veiled language. With reservation, Mary accepts her role as mother of the Son of God. She then describes the coming of her son in terms of food. In hymnic form (The Magnificat) Mary declares that "[God] has filled the hungry with good things" (1:53a). Jesus is born. Then ironically this Jesus, who is to fill the hungry with good things, is actually placed in a feeding trough after his birth (2:7). From the place where animals find nourishment, Jesus begins to provide food for the world.

In Luke 5:1-9, Jesus calls the first disciples: Simon Peter, James, and John. They receive their calling after they have been told by Jesus where to find an enormous catch of fish. After working all night, the disciples have caught nothing. Jesus notices the weary fishermen and gets into a boat. He tells the disciples where to cast their nets. They listen and follow. Soon they have so many fish that their nets begin to break. The story reveals that just as Jesus has the power to feed his disciples, so will the disciples have the ability to feed others. Jesus says to Simon, "Do not be afraid; from now on you will be catching people" (5:10).

The Second Movement: 5–20

In the second and longest movement of Luke's Gospel, Jesus is no longer host but becomes a dinner guest. The first dinner as recorded in Luke's Gospel presents Jesus as the dinner guest in the house of Levi, the tax collector (5:27-32). Levi prepares a great feast in Jesus' honor and invites a large company of tax collectors and others to join them. This first table shows us not only of Jesus' love for eating and being with people, but also of Jesus' lack of concern for social and religious propriety. Jesus shares a table with people who are considered unclean by traditional religious society.

69

Animosity was strong against tax collectors in the first-century world. Tax collectors were Jews who were accused of belonging to the oppressive Roman government. Jewish tax collectors were accused of betraying their own people so that they might gain wealth. They were despised not only for their lack of political allegiance, but also because they were suspected of dishonesty. Their social status in the early first-century world of Judaism was comparable to the immoral reputation of managers of pigeon races and dice-players. They were not given civil rights; they could not be witnesses in legal trials. They were considered unclean. Repentance was only possible if they were willing to leave their occupation.

For Jesus to eat with such folk was to defile religious convention. Jesus broke the religious code and ate with these despised men. It mattered not that these men were considered to be dishonest, guilty of treason, and without hope of repentance. They were the people with whom Jesus chose to party. After dinner, when he was questioned about his lack of social propriety and religious convictions, Jesus proclaimed: "I have come to call not the righteous but sinners to repentance" (5:32). When Jesus was the guest at Levi's table, he was not only finding physical nourishment from the lavish feast, but he was also fulfilling his calling. That calling was to eat food and to experience fellowship at the table with people who had been placed outside the religious structures.

In this second movement as well as in the entire book of Luke, the symbol of food functions like a code. Food describes the new community of God. The old kingdom as represented by John the Baptist had strict rules for responding to food. Often, they were required to fast (5:33). Jesus and the disciples, however, do not follow the dietary laws and are considered spiritually inferior to John the Baptist's movement. But the new life of faith cannot be confined to the traditional dietary laws. The lesson from the vineyard illustrates that new wine simply cannot be placed in old wineskins. If one attempts to recycle the old wineskins, the wine and the skins will be destroyed. The new life of faith is described in terms of wine and food.

The crowds obviously cannot make the new distinctions between food and righteousness. Jesus describes them as "children sitting in the marketplace and calling to one another" (7:32). With their inaccurate, childlike perceptions, they think that John the Baptist, who came eating no bread and drinking no wine, has a demon. Yet they call the one who has come eating and drinking a glutton and a drunkard, a friend of tax collectors and sinners. Their judgments are inconsistent. The crowds do not understand the food code.

Their resentment toward Jesus' dietary customs does not keep Jesus from the table, however. This time Jesus eats with a Pharisee (7:36). Again, Jesus is invited to be the guest in the home of his host. He takes his place at the table and, while there, a woman—considered a sinner by the religious system—breaks cultural conventions and enters a room filled with men and washes Jesus' feet. The table is getting larger. The portrait of Jesus must include characters who represent tax collectors, Pharisees, and women. They all belong at the table with Jesus.

The dinner invitations keep coming. Jesus is the guest in the home of Martha and Mary (10:38-42). While waiting for the meal to be served, Jesus teaches Mary. The radicality of the pre-dinner conversation is easy to miss in our contemporary readings. Jesus is breaking with tradition again. The culture decreed that rabbis should not teach women, and that women were not to be instructed by men. Yet Jesus, while waiting for the meal to be served, teaches Mary. The evangelist Luke makes no apology for Jesus' infraction against the religious tradition. Perhaps good home-cooked meals have a way of overcoming theological barriers and dismantling outdated traditions regarding gender relations.

When Jesus is the dinner guest in the house of a Pharisee (11:37), he continues to defy the standards of religious sensitivity. Just as he resists the status quo and teaches a woman while dinner is being prepared, he also breaks the cleanliness code that was so crucial to the structure of Judaism. He does not wash his hands before dinner (11:39). The Pharisee cannot believe that Jesus would break the rules in such a dramatic fashion. Jesus' response to this host cuts straight to the heart of the matter: "Now you Pharisees clean the outside of the cup and of the dish, but inside you are full of greed and wickedness" (11:39). Jesus' lack of hygiene becomes a lesson in spiritual development. Before the meal is over, Jesus has successfully offended all the dinner guests, both lawyer and Pharisee (11:42-52).

But Jesus continues to receive invitations for dinner, even from the Pharisees. He is invited to a Sabbath meal at the home of a ruler of the Pharisees (14:1-6). Their conversation around the table focuses on food and table manners. At this Sabbath meal, Jesus uses parables to teach the Pharisees and lawyers, who are watching him closely, "lying in wait for him, to catch him in something he might say" (11:54).

These parables highlight Jesus' use of food and banquets as metaphors for understanding discipleship. How should a true disciple live? Jesus notes the discriminatory positioning of guests at the table of the host and gives a lesson on table etiquette from the perspective of the new community of faith. Jesus gives two principles for the new table of God: One, when you are invited to a marriage feast, do not sit at the place of honor. Jesus offers a simple standard, though one contrary to social custom. Social custom required a complex seating arrangement for meals.[3] Because eating together was something more of a ritual or ceremony, one had to position oneself for the evening with great care. Certain seats were assigned based on one's social status. Jesus subverts the custom, however. Rather than competing for the most honorable couch at the table, Jesus says that the guest should take the most humble position at the table.

The second principle for table etiquette in the new community of faith is to throw away your traditional guest lists. In the first century, table fellowship across social lines was rare. It was not appropriate for persons of wealth and rank to be seen eating with persons of lower rank. But once again Jesus subverts the system and declares that the rich host should invite poor guests, that the higher class invite the lower class, that the healthy invite the maimed, blind, and lame to the party.

The table becomes even larger. The new community of God is available for all people.

The word is out. Jesus' ministry is now being defined by his table manners. As the tax collectors and sinners are drawing near to him, the Pharisees and scribes are murmuring, "This fellow welcomes sinners and eats with them" (15:1-2).

The lessons are clear. To be without God is to be hungry, even when the table is filled with food. As the young son leaves home with all his wealth, a famine occurs (15:11-24). In the midst of his accumulation and rebellion, he becomes hungry and must eat scraps of food intended for the hogs. He goes home, starving for food and for God. The father greets him, offers restoration, and prepares a meal. The meal symbolizes the lavish redemption offered by God, the host, given without hesitation, and filled with joy.

In contrast, a rich man, clothed in purple, feasts sumptuously every day (16:19-31). He has food but is without God. A poor man named Lazarus wants to eat whatever might fall from the rich man's table. Even though the rich man's table is full, he dies and lives in perpetual torment. Lazarus, however, dies and lives in perpetual comfort.

The Third Movement: 21–24

In the third movement of Luke's culinary delight, Jesus again becomes the host. The faint, distant tones of the first movement now become loud, melodic patterns as Jesus clearly reveals that he has come to feed the world. His views on table fellowship have led him to this dramatic moment. Now his death is near: "When the hour came, he took his place at the table, and the apostles with him. He said to them, 'I have eagerly desired to eat this Passover with you before I suffer' " (22:14-15).

Jesus serves the cup, then the bread. Yet even the disciples misunderstand the symbols of food. Right after the meal, they begin to argue about positions at the table (22:24-30). Jesus explains that to eat and drink with Jesus is to share in his suffering. The disciples are silent.

Jesus dies. The Food for the World appears to be gone. The party looks as if it is over. Jesus the Host hangs on a cross, not even able to take care of his own thirst. He makes a request for water, but the soldiers mock him and give him vinegar to drink (23:36). But a Pharisee, maybe one with whom Jesus had shared a table of food, Joseph of Arimathea, takes Jesus' body and places it in a tomb. On the first day of the week, the women come to the tomb, see the risen Lord, and go to tell the others. Of course, the disciples do not believe them (24:11). But Jesus the Host continues to search for table guests.

The Coda: 24

The composition comes to a formal close with one more bold spotlight on the theme of food. Jesus appears to two disciples walking on the road to Emmaus (24:12-35). Jesus tries to convince them that he is the Christ, but they do not fully understand until Jesus eats with them (24:27). After much conversation, they invite Jesus to be their dinner guest for it is getting late in the evening (24:29). It is while Jesus breaks the bread that their eyes are opened and they recognize him (24:31). They then go to tell the others. They are careful to describe that Jesus was made known to them in the hospitality of the table—the breaking of the bread (24:35).

It was a meal! Jesus was killed because he used a simple dining table in radical and subversive ways, upsetting the religious system and their prescribed religious codes of table etiquette. Now Jesus uses food to show that he is the Risen Master Host. Although the table killed him, the table now serves as the medium through which disciples can see God.

But the revelation is not to be that easy. As always, there are some skeptics in the crowd. "How can this be the Risen Lord?" they wonder. To their doubts, both visible and hidden, Jesus calls out one more time, "Anybody got anything to eat?" A piece of fish appears, perhaps taken from the catch of the day. Jesus takes the fish and eats it (24:41-43). In this ordinary moment of eating, an epiphany occurs one more time. As we have begun to expect, God is made known by the ordinary act

74

of eating food. In Luke, God does not appear as a majestic burning bush, mighty hurricane winds, or loud claps of thunder. God appears in tables of food and nets of fish caught by his disciples. The followers know God by the way that Jesus eats.

The Portrait of the Community

Much has been written on the identification of the setting of Luke's Gospel. The interpretive options range from a community in severe political distress to a group of wealthy believers trying to learn how to use their financial resources wisely.

Some scholars contend that political strife was at the center of the community's concern. From both Jewish and Roman forces, the community experienced persecution, harassment, and distress. While the Roman government and its anti-Christian position posed the major threat, some contend that the Jewish contingent was also placing pressure on the Lukan community of believers. The first-century reader would have been comforted to know: "When you hear of wars and insurrections, do not be terrified; for these things must take place first, but the end will not follow immediately. . . . By your endurance you will gain your souls" (21:9, 19).

In *Jesus, Politics, and Society*, however, Richard Cassidy argues that Luke's Gospel was never intended to be a political apologetic, but an attempt to make peace with the existing social order. At the heart of the community, says Cassidy, was social strife—not external political threat. The social condition in the Lukan community is described by some writers as one of conflict between the rich and the poor. The Lukan church, primarily composed of wealthy members, struggled to understand the meaning of their wealth and their faith. Their stories are documented in the story of the rich young ruler and Zacchaeus, the wealthy tax collector (Luke 18:18-30; 19:1-10).

In light of this rendering, however, a wider description of Luke's community must be offered. If the table motif is Luke's primary portrait of Jesus, then the community experiences greater social tension than that which can simply be described

75

in political or economic terms. The people sitting around the table are neither Roman soldiers nor wealthy officials of the empire, but people representing various social orders—women, lawyers, tax collectors, Pharisees. I contend that the members of the Lukan congregation are troubled by the existing social condition of first-century society. They are more concerned about the response of Christianity to the various layers of social strata than their fear of political persecution from the Roman government or decisions regarding their money.

The traditional power structures are directly challenged by a Jesus who eats with Pharisees and tax collectors, who fails to wash his hands before he eats, and allows women to join the men in the dining room. This narrative, which highlights Jesus at a table eating and drinking with all kinds of folk, is a testimony to the Lukan community's struggle to find ways to resolve the tension between their new faith and societal structures. For example, if culture, particularly religious culture, has taught, both overtly and covertly, that you should relate socially only with those who look like you, talk like you, and observe the same dietary laws as you, then you are in for a rude awakening when faced with the picture of Jesus who comes breaking all of the societal customs by eating and drinking with outcasts.

Granted, political strife and confusion over a theology of wealth may have contributed to the disequilibrium of the community, but the community was suffering most with the issue of whom to invite over for Sunday dinner. The theological disruption of the community is the heart of the Gospel's message: Throw away your old guest list; Jesus has come as host and guest to the party, and new people have to be added. And that is not easy, especially when the guest list has been handed down for many generations and the social structure depends on who is invited and who is left out.

A partial picture of the Lukan community begins to emerge. A group of believers who lived in an urban center around 85 surround this Gospel. There are both Jews and Gentiles in the congregation. They are financially stable, not the poor Jews of the early Jesus movement. They are struggling with what it means to be a community of faithful believers. Social tensions exist. Members of the community are living in that uncomfortable moment between what used to be and what is going to be. They begin to sense that their old ways of structuring life are antithetically opposed to the new way of life that Jesus Christ has proposed. Because they are products of first-century, class-conscious society, members have a tendency to look down on others who do not belong to their particular class. The culture has taught that classes— professional, ethnic, gender—must remain separate.

They live in an urban center where class distinctions are extremely important for the structuring of the society. Graduations of classes become less important in rural environments where everyone shares the same agricultural concern. Clues from the text identify the urban context of Luke's Gospel. Luke describes houses that belong more likely to a city rather than the countryside. Furthermore, Jesus' sayings reflect concern over future persecution in the cities, excluding Jerusalem (12:11-12). The opposition is from synagogues and city authorities, not from Roman rulers and Sanhedrin leaders belonging to the structure of the city of Jerusalem. Which city? Antioch? Ephesus? It is impossible to know the actual city. The best we can do is to attempt to describe some universal characteristics of urban settings in the first-century world, with particular attention to meals and hospitality.[4]

Meals in antiquity represented more than simply an occasion to enjoy food. Meals were predictable events in the culture that affirmed and legitimated social roles and statuses in the community. Dinners were special ceremonies used to cement social relations. Strict rules governed the ceremony. The position of one's seat was crucial. To sit in the center of the room between the host and the least honorable guest was the preferred seat of honor. Furthermore, table fellowship across status lines was rare. It was culturally taboo for the elite of society to be seen eating in public with persons of lower rank. This societal convention was especially important for the urban dwellers where status stratification was sharp.

Members of the city's elite citizens were expected to maintain the cultural divisions.

The community of Luke's Gospel painted its picture of Jesus at a table, eating and drinking with all kinds of people, because persons of Luke's community were struggling to relate their new faith with their old culture. Three layers of cultural confusion existed in the community of Luke's Gospel.

First, should the church embrace people of another race? Conflict in the Lukan community emerged when law-observant Christian Jews were expected to eat church fellowship dinners with non-Jews. This would have been no small problem, for the social barriers separating the races were probably the greatest at the table. Food for the Jews required special preparation and utensils. Some foods were to be avoided. Special rituals were a prerequisite to eating the meal. To eat with people who did not follow the same concerns regarding food created enormous problems. The community struggled with this issue. They found solutions as they remembered Jesus, who chose not to follow the laws of the table, choosing instead to eat with everyone, even tax collectors and sinners, and who at times did not even wash his hands.

Second, the church struggled with the question: Should the church accept women? In Luke, women are associated with food and meals (4:38-39; 7:36-50; 10:38-42). In most references the women assume an inferior role, most often found in servants rather than in leadership roles (4:38-39; 7:36-40; 10:38-42). In 7:36-50, Jesus opens the door of the dining room to a woman. Contradicting societal and religious standards, a woman, who also happens to be a sinner, enters a room where Jesus and Simon, a Pharisee, are having dinner. By societal standards, women did not join men at the table. Furthermore, sinners did not associate with Pharisees. This bold woman disregards the tradition and anoints Jesus' feet with ointment. Jesus, likewise, disregards those same standards and praises her for her genuine kindness, all the while chiding his Pharisee host for his lack of hospitality. Life is simply more when Jesus is at the table.

78

Third, the Lukan congregation may have been facing the question: Should the members of the church cross social status lines? Social tensions existed between the elite and the poor of society. Luke's interest in meals suggests that the persons of the community centered around the Gospel were also interested in meals, culture, and faith. For example, Jesus urges the host of the meal to go find the "poor, the crippled, the lame, and the blind" (14:13). The prospective guests are defined by their social location. They are those without money, education, and social status. The Lukan community hears Jesus' voice, "Do not invite your friends or your brothers or your relatives or rich neighbors, in case they may invite you in return, and you would be repaid" (14:12). In other words, invite those not from your own economic circle, choose those who cannot afford to reciprocate. Break with the system that divides classes by money. Provide free hospitality to everyone.

The Portrait of the Reader

Luke's portrait of Jesus is clear in Luke's Gospel. Jesus comes eating and drinking, redefining the table and life for the people of faith. The portrait of the community is also clear. Luke's congregation focuses its story of Jesus around a table. The narrative stands as a monument to the struggles with dinner guest lists and Christian table etiquette. Persons in Luke's community struggle with the requirement of open table fellowship in the new community of faith. Should the table be small and only include selected, righteous guests? Or should the table be large enough to include those from different social positions, races, or genders? As the Lukan church wrestles with these social and theological issues, it shapes a portrait of Jesus that features a huge dining room table with dinner guests from everywhere. And as we read the narrative, we see their struggle and the final resolution as they determine that the table of Christ is for everyone.

Where do we fit in? What self-portrait do we unveil as we view Luke's picture of Jesus? Our portrait is not unlike that of the community, I am afraid. For we as a church are still struggling with the very same issues of inclusivity. We still wrestle with the same social/theological issue: Who should be at the table, and whom should we exclude?

Some of us are like the crowds who simply cannot believe that the Gospel includes the ordinary events of eating and drinking. We look for higher places to portray theological thought. We shine our theological documents because we think that the gospel can best be enshrined there. We develop lofty mission statements because we think that truth can best be described in what we say rather than what we do. We establish elaborate ecclesiastical systems because we think that God will most comfortably reside within our structures. We are not unlike the crowds in Luke's narrative who simply cannot understand that the simple acts of eating and drinking can belong to the new community of faith. "It is too simple, too nontheological, too common," we explain. God certainly would not reveal God's self at an ordinary dining room table with common food. Little do we realize that it is at the kitchen table where the best theological formulations are developed.

Maybe we share the same portrait as the Pharisees. We know the power of the table because we have been taught from our childhood that it matters a great deal with whom you share a meal. So we remember meals, some prepared at the back of Woolworth's store for one racial grouping and other meals prepared at the front of the store for another one. We remember how races were divided at public water fountains and restrooms. In our current political correctness we defy those ancient lines of demarcation and protest loudly against racial discrimination. Not unlike those Pharisees, although we talk well, we do not mingle socially with those who are not of our race. We do not seem to invite those who are not of our color over to watch the football game and eat pizza on Saturday afternoon. Sunday morning worship remains the most segregated hour of the week. We prefer to eat and worship with our own race. Although soda counters, water fountains, and restrooms no longer divide us, the division continues to reside in our hearts and in the simple practices of our daily lives.

Or maybe we wear the face of the Pharisee who challenges Jesus' authority because he allows a woman to enter the dining room and wash his feet. It is not just the first-century world that placed women in inferior positions in society. Considered unclean by the first-century Jewish tradition, estimation of women in twentieth-century culture is not much higher. Women are considered inferior, less intelligent, and incapable of providing executive leadership. According to the Gospel of Luke, however, the table is open to everyone. Social discourse, business conversation, and certainly teachings about the life of faith occur at the table. And women are to be included.

Perhaps we find our face in the character of the host who learns how to revise his guest list (14:15-24). After several unsuccessful attempts to invite the "right" people to his banquet, the host gives up and sends his servants into the highways and hedges to invite whoever will come to the party. How many times have we planned social occasions and invited only those who belonged to our certain group? How many of us have been willing to include those people who would not normally appear on anyone's guest list?

Our faces are painted in the narrative of Luke's Gospel. We see our own inability to sit at the table with others of God's children. May these portraits convince us of our need to repent and then empower us to follow Jesus' example at the table.

Notes

[1]C. H. Talbert, *Reading Luke: A Literary and Theological Commentary on the Third Gospel* (New York: The Crossroad Publishing Co., Inc., 1986) 7-11.

[2]Robert J. Karris, *Luke: Artist and Theologian: Luke's Passion Account as Literature* (New York: Paulist Press, 1985) 47.

[3]Bruce J. Malina and Richard L. Rohrbaugh, *Social-Science Commentary on the Synoptic Gospels* (Minneapolis MN: Fortress Press, 1992).

[4]Halvor Moxnes, "The Social Context of Luke's Community," *Interpretation* 48 (1994): 383-89.

For Further Reading

Corley, Kathleen. *Private Women, Public Meals: Social Conflict in the Synoptic Tradition.* Peabody MA: Hendrickson Publishers, Inc., 1993.

Karris, Robert J. *Luke: Artist and Theologian.* New York: Paulist Press, 1985.

Kingsbury, Jack Dean. *Conflict in Luke: Jesus, Authorities, Disciples.* Minneapolis MN: Fortress Press, 1991.

Neyrey, Jerome H., ed. *The Social World of Luke-Acts.* Peabody MA: Hendrickson Publishers, Inc., 1991.

Talbert, C. H. *Reading Luke: A Literary and Theological Commentary on the Third Gospel.* New York: The Crossroad Publishing Co., Inc., 1982.

Chapter 4

The Portrait of Jesus
in John

From a new color palette and school of portraiture come the shades, strokes, and content for the portrait of Jesus in the Gospel of John. John replaces the somber, dark colors of the Markan portrait with vibrant shades of light. Jesus' Jewish rabbinic garb, painted so carefully in Matthew's Gospel, fades into the background in John's portrait. Johannine sacred spaces of fig trees, wells, and temple porticoes supplant familiar Lucan dining room tables. The Johannine canvas, filled with light, portrays people—Nathanael, Nicodemus, the Samaritan woman, religious leaders, Mary and Martha, Lazarus, the blind man and others. Their eyes are fixed on Jesus, the Light, who stands in the center of the painting.

The people painted on the canvas appear to be moving. Like the flickering motion of a hologram, the Johannine characters change locations. Some move from darkness to light, disorder to order, and confusion to clarity; others move from light to dark, from understanding to rejection. We see transformations of people in John's portrait. The theological description of the positive change is conversion, a change in attitude, life focus, and eternal destiny. The official portrait title lifted from the Gospel's Prologue states: "But to all who received him, who believed in his name, he gave power to become children of God" (1:12). The portrait of Jesus in John can be simply labeled, Jesus saves.

The Spiritual Gospel

While a foreign missionary in Taiwan, I read the Gospel of John with Chinese young people around my kitchen table in Taipei. I remember choosing this Gospel for the group of non-Christians because I thought that it was the easiest to understand. I knew that most Bible societies chose to translate the Gospel of John first. I also knew that the Gospel was often distributed in individual tracts or pamphlets for non-Christians. I chose it for our reading group because of its simplicity. The meaning of John's Gospel was easy to understand, or so I thought.

Later I spent several years combing through stacks of books and articles written on John, preparing to write a dissertation. I saw the complexity and the lack of agreement among scholars concerning the Gospel's meaning. Faced with both the simplicity and profundity, I agreed with the scholar who said that the Gospel of John was shallow enough for a child to wade in and deep enough for an elephant to swim in. This wonderful Gospel is simple enough for young Chinese inquirers, yet deep enough for tons of scholarly research. This Gospel is special.

The early church was also fascinated with the Gospel of John. By 180, early writers attributed the Gospel to the work of John the son of Zebedee and Beloved Disciple, establishing apostolic status and thus securing a position within the canon. Although accepted by the center of the church, the Gospel of John was also a favorite of a group of people in the margins, known as the Gnostics. The Gnostics posed a great threat to the tradition with their lack of orthodoxy, and with time, lessened the credibility of the Fourth Gospel.

The Gospel of John became the center of theological controversy by the second and third century. *The Gospel of Truth*, a second-century gnostic writing from Egypt, shows extensive parallels to the Gospel of John. Heracleon, a famous disciple of Valentinus who founded a gnostic sect, wrote the first commentary on the Gospel of John. Montanus proclaimed that he was the coming Paraclete as described in John 14–16. The church later used the Gospel to support christological debates.

While some leaders read the Gospel to advocate Jesus' humanity, Athanasius and the Council of Nicea (325) used the Fourth Gospel to support Jesus' divinity.

Eusebius, writing in the beginning of the fourth century, preserved a comment made by Clement of Alexandria (200): "John, last of all, conscious that the outward facts had been set forth in the Gospels, was urged on by his disciples, and, divinely moved by the Spirit, composed a spiritual Gospel." This spiritual Gospel was influential in the church from Augustine to Aquinas.

With the advent of the Enlightenment of the eighteenth century, the Gospel's historical character was challenged. Spiritual meant ahistorical for many scholars writing during the age of reason. Scholars who were looking for a more historical, less spiritual account of Jesus challenged the historicity of the Gospel of John. The best example of nineteenth-century skepticism was written by K. G. Bretschneider, a German pastor, who wrote:

> It is not possible that both the Jesus of the first three Gospels and the Jesus of the Fourth Gospel are historically true at the same time . . . it is also not possible that the first three evangelists invented Jesus' teaching, morals, and way of teaching; the author of the Fourth Gospel could quite possibly have concocted his Jesus.[1]

Although others opposed this position, the age of reason had dawned, leaving the Fourth Gospel sitting alone and isolated from the other three Gospels. Matthew, Mark, and Luke were reliable, but John lacked authenticity, the scholars said.

Even though the historical veracity of the Fourth Gospel has been challenged by scholars, this Gospel remains prominent in the hearts and minds of followers of Christ in the late twentieth century. People still want to read the Fourth Gospel. Scholars are still sifting through the tons of scholarly research and finding new approaches to reading John's narrative. The Gospel has power to communicate. A few years ago, I taught the Gospel of John in thirteen churches in ten weeks. People came each night to learn more about what many of them said was their favorite book in the Bible. The Age of Enlightenment had not removed this challenging story from the New Testament canon nor from the hands of the people.

The uniqueness of John's portrait does not make it less reliable. That the Fourth Evangelist paints with a different brush, uses different lighting and colors, and sees the primary figure of Christ from a unique perspective does not lessen the authenticity of this Gospel. Perhaps it will be in the next century, when extreme polarities of faith and reason cease to exist, that we will be able to appreciate fully the Fourth Gospel. Without the rigid categories of historical and ahistorical we may be able to comprehend more fully the truth represented in this awesome Gospel.

A former student from Union Theological Seminary in Virginia, Lynn Miller, now a Presbyterian minister, artist, and historian, gave me a new way to describe the historical and spiritual dimensions of the Fourth Gospel. In a paper required for New Testament class, she compared the style of portraiture in the Fourth Gospel to the paintings of nineteenth-century Impressionism. She wrote that impressionism was not antithetical to realism, for actual objects were still important to the impressionist painter. The major distinction between the two schools of art was in the use of light. impressionists were fascinated by variations of light on surrounding objects. Rather than emphasize the actual objects as in realism, the impressionist painter used small strokes of unmixed primary colors to simulate actual reflected light. Miller wrote:

> Until the time of the Impressionists, painters worked almost exclusively in their studios. The Impressionists chose to take their paints, brushes, and canvasses out into the light and paint *en plein air*, believing that they could capture the fleeting impressions of light only by being out in the light.[2]

For example, Monet painted *Rouen Cathedral in the Afternoon* without the delicate pinks and blues of the morning but with various shades of yellow. The purpose was not to highlight the flowers or the shape of the building. The purpose was to show the power of light as it reflects the ever-changing effects on the surroundings.

Monet, an impressionist painter of the late 1800s, made an art of the instantaneous. Because he shifted the focus of art from shapes to light, he nor his work were initially accepted by the fashionable art salons of Paris. His novel approach ignored the traditional, studied responses to shape and design, and he chose to paint light instead. The task was not easy, because the scene was constantly changing depending on the time of day and the weather conditions, but Monet remained committed to this new art form.

Harbors, haystacks, gardens, and cathedrals were simply the background for the central focus of his paintings—the light. Daniel Boorstin describes Monet's work: "Of all painters' works, those of Monet are hardest to describe in words, precisely because they had no 'subject' but the momentary visual impression on a unique self."[3] Monet's friend, George Clemenceau, declared that the impressions of the Rouen Cathedral were revolutionary, that they were truly a hymn celebrating the cathedral as a mirror for the unfolding works of light in time. This ability to capture the light, the speediest messenger of the senses, moved Clemenceau to write to Monet, "I love you, because you are you, and because you taught me to understand light."[4]

The Fourth Gospel is like that. The Light of the World takes central focus. The realistic shapes of structured buildings, chronological time lines, and historical diaries fade to the background, and the Light of the World takes central space. The Fourth Evangelist takes Jesus' synoptic portrait out into the light, much like the style of the impressionist painters. Like the work of Monet, the community of John's Gospel presents Jesus' portrait as a study of light that is not limited to historical details. The historical details are important in the story only in the way they reflect the Light. The Johannine community takes the portrait of Jesus out of the studio and *en plein air* and, with small brushstrokes shows us how Jesus, the Light, changed its environment.

The Portrait of Jesus

When you freely associate with the phrase, "Jesus saves," what do you see? What do you hear? I see the man in the football stadium who holds the John 3:16 sign at every televised ballgame. I hear the street evangelists in the little mountain town of my youth who stood on the corner of Main Street, Bible raised to the sky, every Saturday morning shouting to all who would listen, "Jesus saves." I recall humid, sticky, August evenings in the mountains of North Carolina, sitting under the wooden tabernacle at camp meeting time. The preacher managed to get the attention of the teenagers sitting way in the back when he would yell at the top of his lungs, "Jesus saves." I think of fall revivals in country churches that began the service each night with a rousing musical call to worship, "We have heard the joyful sound . . . Jesus saves, Jesus saves."

Those images are dated now. We laugh at the sign during the ballgame, almost embarrassed at the public display. We rarely hear of summer camp meetings anymore. The hymn, "Jesus Saves," remains at the back of the hymnal and usually at the end of the choir's repertoire. These words and events speak of another time, another era when public testimonies, long altar calls, and packed pews were expected, remnants of the old-time religion.

For the postmodern Christian, "Jesus saves" connotes high-pressured evangelistic strategies, unreasonable and unclear synopses of numbered spiritual laws, and ineffective ballgame posters and car bumper stickers. We are faced with a dilemma. To use the phrase is to confuse potential listeners; yet, to omit it loses the full significance of John's portrait. To ignore this powerful portrait of change, of Jesus' power to save, would be a great loss to the church's portrait gallery. The portrait is a good one and one worth reclaiming for the contemporary church.

Although we may have discarded the word in the modern church, we have not lost it in our daily lives. We speak of *saving* coupons to reduce our grocery bill or *saving* newspapers to recycle. We *save* money in order to send our children to college

88

or to buy a new home. Occasionally the newspaper uses the word *saves* to report a dramatic rescue from fire or flood. The word still communicates. Why lose it?

To save means "to rescue from harm, danger, or loss; to keep in a safe condition; to prevent the waste or loss of; to treat with care in order to avoid fatigue, wear, or damage." The Gospel of John shows just that. Jesus saves people from loss, keeps them in a safe condition, and treats them with utmost care. Episode after episode, John reveals characters who encounter Jesus and then are changed. Jesus saves in John.

The People

The first twelve chapters of the Gospel of John include a narrative roll call of people who respond to Jesus. Personalities such as Nicodemus, the Samaritan woman, and the blind man are unique to John's Gospel; we know the others from reading the Synoptics, such as the disciples, Mary, Jesus' mother, religious leaders, and the crowds.[5] These people are in the story for one purpose—to respond to Jesus. We watch them carefully. Some of these folk will reject Jesus' offer of salvation. Some will only secretly believe. Others will follow Jesus and experience a dramatic change in their lives. They are the objects in Jesus' portrait who receive the brilliant trajectories of light.

The prologue (1:1-18) describes the primary focus of light in the portrait. Jesus' power resides with God and manifests a cosmic dimension (1:1-3). In Christ resides life. That life becomes the light for all of us, in spite of the darkness (1:4-5). What a beautiful beginning! This is sheer poetry, with images that cannot be expressed in squares and rectangles of concrete buildings and historical edifices but only in dramatic explosions of light.

To describe what the Light is requires a description of what the Light is not. The poetic flow of the prologue is interrupted by a parenthetical note, which states clearly that the Light is not John the Baptist. (1:6-8) As helpful as his ministry was to God's plan of salvation, the Baptist was only a witness to the Light. The true Light that was able to shine on all people came into the world through Christ (1:9-11).

One of the most tragic verses in the entire Bible follows: "He came to what was his own, and his own people did not accept him" (1:11). The cross of Jesus is written over these words, as well as his physical and emotional isolation from family and friends. Deeply embedded in the Incarnation is Good Friday. Because of the Incarnation, however, the tragedy of Good Friday turns to triumph even for the observers. The remaining phrase completes the story: "But to all who received him, who believed in his name, he gave power to become children of God" (1:12). Jesus' power to save is ultimately connected to his power to suffer. The prologue announces that Good Friday always precedes Easter morning. The power is God's, the agent is Christ, and we are the recipients. God saves us through Jesus Christ.

The Incarnation announces that God came in the flesh and stayed (1:14). The Johannine good news is that the Incarnation never grows old, nor does the Light ever give out. The God who came in flesh resides with us in Spirit. Abiding, resting, remaining, making tabernacle, and being vine and branches all are Johannine communicative devices used to announce that God, who created the world, stays around to watch over the creation. Although we have never seen God, the Incarnate One has made God known (1:18).

The prologue is to the narrative as an overture is to a musical composition. As an overture introduces the musical themes to be heard throughout the composition, the first eighteen verses of John introduce us to the great themes of John's narrative. From this Gospel overture, we know that the full portrait will represent Light and people, those who believe and others who reject. A former student said that reading the prologue is like peeling an onion. The more you peel, the more there is to peel. We go now to find other layers of this story that reveal a God who comes in the form of Jesus Christ to offer life to people.

Christological identity is an issue that cannot be neglected by the portrait (1:19-34). In the first century, many messiahs traveled the land promising new life, but the Fourth Evangelist knew only one—Jesus Christ. Some of the followers thought that John the Baptist was the Messiah. The Fourth Evangelist makes sure that the readers know that Jesus is the Christ, not the Baptist. The Baptist knows Jesus Christ and says, "Here is the Lamb of God who takes away the sin of the world" (1:29). The Incarnation comes attached with a mission statement. It is not enough just to provide a continual presence in the world; the Light must also take away the sin of the world.

The Baptist also provides a model for leadership. He is a voice crying out in the wilderness, preparing the way for the Lord, who is not worthy even to untie Jesus' sandals. His servant nature is exemplified when he encourages his own followers to follow the Lamb of God (1:35). At least two followers of John the Baptist become Jesus' disciples (1:37-42). Andrew belongs to the collection of characters whose lives are changed because of the Light (1:40). Leave room on the canvas for Simon, the son of John, who is Andrew's brother. Simon, called Cephas, even receives a name change to indicate his newfound status. Andrew changes leaders, and Simon's name is changed.

Philip also belongs to the portrait of people whose lives have been changed because of Jesus (1:43-44). Nathanael is not so compliant, however (1:45-51). The skeptic takes his time before he recognizes the Light shining in this face. At first, Nathanael resists. Jesus' omniscience convinces Nathanael that this one who called him while he was studying the Torah under the fig tree is actually God. Nathanael's life is changed. Jesus promises Nathanael that, if he will believe, he will see even "greater things than these" (1:50-51). Nathanael leaves the fig tree and follows Jesus.

Add some party people to the collection of characters for the canvas (2:1-12). We do not know all of their names: a steward, a bride, a bridegroom, Mary, Jesus' mother, the disciples, and other guests. Jesus turns water into wine, and the disciples believed. Even water is changed when Jesus is present.

Another group belongs in the painting: the religious leaders. They see the Light, but choose not to live in the Light. We are first introduced to them after Jesus cleanses the temple. Jesus responds to their demand for a sign to validate his authority. Yet, they show their confusion when Jesus says, "Destroy this temple, and in three days I will raise it up" (2:19). They think that Jesus is talking about the temple building, but we know, because of the voice of the narrator in the text, that Jesus speaks of his impending death and resurrection (2:21). The religious leaders misunderstand the Light.

One of their leaders named Nicodemus, however, goes to Jesus for clarification (3:1-21). Somewhat brave, somewhat scared, Nicodemus comes to Jesus in the night and says, "Rabbi, we know that you are a teacher who has come from God; for no one can do these signs that you do apart from the presence of God" (3:2). Nicodemus is searching for the Light.[6] While trying diligently to analyze the Light, Nicodemus misses the beauty of its rays. Nicodemus ponders, "How can anyone be born after having grown old?" Jesus explains that birth from above is more than what one can see with earthly vision (3:5-14). Eternal life is given by God through Christ (3:16-18). The Light has come, exposing sin, providing guidance, and giving life (3:19-21).

Leave space on the canvas for the Samaritan woman, one of my favorite Johannine characters.[7] She carries a pitcher of water on her head, even though her back is burdened by life's cares. She wants to see no one as she walks to the well at high noon when the other women are at home resting in the heat of the day. A conversation with Jesus occurs. The topics of conversation include Samaritan theology, literal and metaphorical water, her personal life, and issues of christology—not your typical, public discourse between a man and a woman. Public conversations between a man and a woman are taboo, and relationships between Jews and Samaritans are prohibited.

She has had broken relationships with five husbands. According to ancient law, the man could break the marriage contract for various reasons, even his wife's lack of cooking skills or natural beauty (Deut 24:1-4). The wife could neither initiate nor contest the divorce. The system of patriarchy has abused the Samaritan woman, leaving her suspicious of men and stripped of her own personal grounding. She has lost hope in the possibility of marriage; she is living with a man who is not her husband.

In the midst of her sadness, Jesus comes and offers her free, running water. The disciples look on with scorn, for Jesus has broken with religious custom by speaking with this woman in public (4:27). Their disapproval does not matter, however, to the woman or to Jesus. Like a chrysalis shedding a cocoon, this woman is about to be changed. John's portrait suggests change by a slight but dramatic narrative aside—she forgets her water jar (4:28). Without this encumbrance, her posture changes, and she runs to tell others what she has discovered. Because of her witness and Jesus' words, they believe (4:39-42).

Couched in the episode of the Samaritan woman is another, although brief, story of Jesus' power to change lives (4:46-54). The son of a royal official is dying. Jesus simply says to the father, "Go; your son will live" (4:50). This event of healing requires no majestic sound effects, no gathered audience, just words. The official believes Jesus' words. The entire family is changed when Jesus heals the son. The official's family believes (4:54).

The picture of people in John must include the man at the pool of Bethesda (5:1-18). This man has been sick for thirty-eight years. He is waiting for someone to help him enter the pool. The portrait reveals the change. Prior to meeting Jesus, he cannot move. After the encounter, the man picks up his pallet and walks away from the pool. Because of Jesus, this man's life is changed.

The hungry crowds also need to be included, but they belong in a place where the Light has been blocked from view (6:1-71). In John, the crowds do not understand the Light. Jesus feeds them, and they want to make him a political king (6:15). Jesus teaches them, and they complain. Not unlike their ancestors in the wilderness, who complained against Moses and Aaron (Exod 16), the crowds grumble extensively and block out the Light. Many followers defect at this point, unwilling to receive the Light: "Because of this many of his disciples turned back and no longer went about with him" (6:66). We are prepared to leave some space dark in the portrait because we know "that the light has come into the world, and people loved darkness rather than light" (3:19).

The crowds continue to complain (7:12). Some think that Jesus has a demon (7:20). Others think that he is a prophet (7:40). Others think that he is the Christ (7:41). The debate continues over Jesus' hometown. Like Nathanael, Jesus' origins become a stumbling block for the crowds. And they cry, "Surely the Messiah does not come from Galilee?" The true Messiah comes from David's city of Bethlehem, they clamor.

A woman at the temple, however, does not care where Jesus was born; his offer of forgiveness is enough (8:1-11). She has committed adultery, according to the scribes and Pharisees. The leaders are preparing to stone her. Jesus stands and says, "Let anyone among you who is without sin be the first to throw a stone at her." Jesus saves this woman. He saves her from loss and treats her with utmost care. She moves from sin into life when Jesus says to her, "Neither do I condemn you. Go your way, and from now on do not sin again" (8:11).

The centrality of light in this impressionistic painting is seen in 8:12-20. Jesus says, "I am the light of the world. Whoever follows me will never walk in darkness but will have the light of life." Again, there are those in the portrait who have moved away from the Light. Because the crowds refuse the Light, they take up stones to throw at him, and the Light leaves the temple (8:59).

Although in the portrait the Light fades from the crowds, in contrast, the Light shines profusely on the man born blind (9:1-40). Filling an entire chapter, this episode emphasizes Jesus' portrait of light. A blind man receives sight because the Light of the World offers him the Light. The episode trembles with excitement, telling the story of physical healing and spiritual conversion. This change of location, from blindness to sight, became the metaphor for the hymn writer, Isaac Newton, who included these words in "Amazing Grace": "I once was blind, but now I see." Jesus saves by rescuing people from loss of sight, both physically and spiritually.

A dramatic change from death to life occurs for Lazarus (11:1-44). The story begins with Jesus' admonishing the listeners:

> Are there not twelve hours of daylight? Those who walk during the day do not stumble, because they see the light of this world. But those who walk at night stumble, because the light is not in them. (11:9-10)

Martha also belongs in this portrait of change. Martha is known in the Synoptics as the resentful, domesticated woman who is overshadowed by her sister's quiet piety. In John, her role is bolder and has more depth. She leaves her passive domesticated role, meets Jesus on the road, and admonishes him for taking so long to come to them in their grief: "Lord, if you had been here, my brother would not have died" (11:21). She knows that Jesus could have helped. Now she must wait until the day of resurrection. As we read the dialogue between Jesus and Martha, we watch the process of change. Martha's understanding of time is radically changed. Initially Martha envisions change only in the future. She knows that Lazarus will rise again in the resurrection at the last day, in the sweet by and by. She learns, however, that her friend Jesus also has the power to change the present. Jesus Christ, in the here and now, can bring her brother to life. Until this point, she has not understood that Jesus, her friend, is truly God. In response, she makes one of the highest christological responses in the entire Gospel when she says, "Yes, Lord, I believe that you are the Messiah, the Son of God, the one coming into the world" (11:27). The Light has power not only to resurrect the dead but to change limited theological understandings of faith. Martha's eschatology changes from a futuristic understanding of the "sweet by and by" to a present reality of God at work in the "nasty here and now."

Chapter 12 summarizes some of the responses to Jesus the Light. Jesus enters Jerusalem. The crowds celebrate. Even the English text labels this paragraph as the "triumphal entry."

Jesus, however, can see no triumph at this point—only impending tragedy.

We hear the responses. The disciples still do not understand (12:16). Even after all these years of being with Jesus, watching him heal others, listening to him teach, hearing him pray, they are still confused. They will understand later (2:22). The crowds, who had watched Lazarus come to life, want to see some more signs. They are captivated by the supernatural and sensational (12:17-18). Ironically, the Pharisees have understood, and they say, "You see, you can do nothing. Look, the world has gone after him" (12:19).

In this final section before the story of Jesus' passion, Jesus warns the crowds,

> The light is with you for a little longer. Walk while you have the light, so that the darkness may not overtake you. If you walk in the darkness, you do not know where you are going. While you have the light, believe in the light, so that you may become children of light. (12:35-36)

The Light

We fill the borders of the Johannine canvas with people, but the center belongs to the Light (12–21). The prophet Isaiah provided the inspiration for the Evangelist's portrayal of Christ: "Arise, shine, for your light has come" (Isa 60:1). The same image was the watchword for Baptist Young Women who worked with a vision of people and their need for the Light. I can still hear the voices of women as their leader, my mother, would begin each meeting with this scriptural reminder of Light.

How do you describe Light? These final chapters give us a clue. Chapters 13–16 record Jesus' final words of farewell. Before Jesus dies, the Light washes people's feet and teaches that this is the model for us all (13:1-20).

Baptist Theological Seminary at Richmond began a towel tradition with our first graduating class in 1992. Every year on the evening before graduation, President Tom Graves presents the real ministerial diplomas to each graduate. They receive a towel with their name inscribed. The seminary acknowledges that the mark of a real minister is not the ability to parse Greek verbs, handle Hebrew exegesis, list major movements in church history, or recite theological confessions, but to wash the feet of people.

To wash feet is a literal sign and a figurative image reflecting the new commandment given by Jesus in the last few hours of his life: "I give you a new commandment, that you love one another. Just as I have loved you, you also should love one another" (13:34-35). This theme does not grow weary on the lips of Jesus in John or in the minds of the church. Jesus says again, "If you love me, you will keep my commandments. . . . Those who love me will keep my word, and my Father will love them, and we will come to them and make our home with them" (14:15, 23). Jesus also says, "As the Father has loved me, so I have loved you; abide in my love. If you keep my commandments, you will abide in my love, just as I have kept my Father's commandments and abide in his love" (15:9). The repetition keeps the message of the Light clearly in focus: "I am giving you these commands," says Jesus, "so that you may love one another" (15:17).

This theme of love continues to echo as Jesus prays to the Father "that they may be one, as we are one" (17:11). Not all choose to be one with God, however. Judas soon leads a group of soldiers and officers of the chief priests and the Pharisees to the disciples' secret meeting place, where Jesus will be arrested (18:2). The Light of the World stands in the garden and, even in these moments before his death, outshines the temporal light of lanterns, torches, and weapons (18:3).

Judas cannot extinguish the Light. Peter cannot diminish the power of the Light through his denial (18:15-27). Pilate cannot protect Christ from those who would try to banish the Light (19:1-16). Jesus Christ, the Light of the World, prepares to die. While the soldiers are deciding how to divide a seamless garment between four people, Jesus is giving his entire life to a small group of people, three women named Mary and a male called the "disciple whom he loved" (19:23-27). The more prominent members are absent, in hiding for fear of their own lives. Those who stay at the cross are willing to die with Jesus. Jesus inaugurates new relationships not formed from blood lines or shared family trees but from the life of Christ, the Light of the World. Mary, the mother of Jesus, and the "disciple whom he loved" are related because of the life and death of Christ.

In the Fourth Gospel, Jesus' death is told simply—no prolonged agony, no sweat drops of blood sorrowing over his future fate, no tumult of nature (19:28-41). Two secret disciples, Joseph of Arimathea and Nicodemus, quietly bury the body.

The resurrection story, however, is told with greater detail, energetically announcing that the Light is not extinguished. Mary Magdalene is the first one to see Jesus. She speaks in this Gospel, unlike her muted voice in the Synoptics. She says to the disciples who have been hiding, "I have seen the Lord" (20:18). Mary's words are not spoken with ambivalence nor in timid declaration. She proclaims (*angelousa*) the message of the Living Light as a heavenly messenger would speak when representing God. Mary announces the resurrection of Jesus Christ. Arise, shine, Mary, for your Light has come.

Simon Peter receives another chance to participate in the Light. As he denied Jesus three times, three times Peter affirms that he loves Jesus. These conversations conclude with Peter's commissioning service. Jesus says to Peter, "Feed my sheep" (21:15-19). Arise, shine, Peter, for your Light has come.

The Fourth Evangelist acknowledges the limitations of the community's portrait: "But there are also many other things that Jesus did; if every one of them were written down, I suppose that the world itself could not contain the books that would be written" (21:25). Although the Johannine canvas is the largest in the gallery, it is not large enough. As we stand and meditate on this Johannine portrait, we remain in awe at the beauty of the Light and its reflection on the faces of the people painted on the canvas. The Light has come. People's lives have been changed. The Johannine portrait reveals clearly that Jesus saves.

The Portrait of the Community

The Gospel of John bears the marks of multiple minds and hands in several editions spanning five decades. The narrative provides the evidence for multiple authorship. First, the closing words of the Beloved Disciple suggest more than one author: "We know that his testimony is true" (21:24). Second, the language of the text suggests a close-knit group of people who shared understanding of unique images, metaphors, and in-house phrases. Third, the fabric of the narrative reveals layers of literary genres and sources, such as signs, discourse, poetry, aphorisms, and passion, that were contributed by several groups of people through time. Finally, the theological tensions within the narrative suggest the work of several people, perhaps even with competing ideologies.

How do you describe such a group of people who left us with this unique portrait of Jesus? What do their writings reveal about them? Obviously, they left no autobiographical material, except this single document. No cornerstone from the first-century Johannine church has been uncovered to reveal important information about the group, for they probably had no official meeting house, except the synagogue in their early days.

The text gives us clues. Although not written to feature the history of the community, the Fourth Gospel bears the imprint of the authors. A description emerges from reading the Fourth Gospel. The Johannine community was diverse theologically and ethnically, egalitarian in structure, and inclined to make exclusive claims about Christ in response to pressure from the Jewish tradition and the Roman government. These three adjectives—diverse, egalitarian, and exclusive—organize our discussion of the Johannine community. This discussion leans heavily on the work of J. L. Martyn, Raymond Brown, Alan Culpepper, and Richard Cassidy.[8]

First, the community of the Fourth Gospel was diverse. In the center of the community a small group of people, perhaps a school or individual persons assigned to the writing task, wrote and edited the final edition (completed in 90) of the Fourth Gospel. The Beloved Disciple was influential in the early years of the school, providing eyewitness reports and important leadership. This school of writers represented a larger population of racially diverse folk, including followers of John the Baptist, secret believers, various Jewish groups, Hellenists, Samaritans, and Gentile converts.

The Johannine community, which originated around 50 in or near Palestine, was also theologically diverse. For three decades (50–80), the community assimilated various viewpoints from their racially diverse constituents. When the Gospel reached its final form in 90, those diverse positions were included in the narrative. The lack of homogeneity, both in race and ideas, attests to an unusual community, one that could maintain community in diversity. The Gospel of John witnesses to the church's ability to maintain theological tension and remain in community with one another, at least for five decades.

The community differed on issues such as christology and eschatology. Some members of the church understood Jesus as the Davidic Messiah (7:42); others viewed Jesus from a Mosaic background (3:14). Some saw Jesus as a great miracle worker (6:14), but others tended to place his words as more important than his deeds (4:50). Some understood Jesus from above, a high christology that identifies the cosmic Christ, high and preexistent (1:1-5). Others understood Christ from below, pointing to his Incarnation—the word that became flesh (1:14). It would be this issue, however, that would split the community into two groups by the year 100. The writing of the Johannine epistles reveal that the tension of two christological positions, Jesus' humanity and divinity, could not be held in tension indefinitely.

Eschatology, however, did not cause the same long-term conflict for the church. Just as the Fourth Gospel does not record a one-sided view of the nature of Christ, a monolithic presentation of eschatology does not exist either. Some passages point to the future as the time of fulfillment, and others clearly state that the time is already here. Condemnation is happening now (3:18), and will also occur in the last day (12:48). Eternal life is given in the present (3:36) and is also available in the future (12:25).

Second, the community was egalitarian. A sense of acceptance pervades the Gospel, particularly the acceptance of women.[9] The women are presented positively, all having close and intimate relationships with Jesus. They are presented as individuals, with clear and evolving personalities. Their characters are not flat but round. Compare the one-dimensional presentation of Nicodemus in chapter 3 with the complex characterization of the Samaritan woman in chapter 4.

The use of Martha is the most revealing piece of evidence for understanding the role of women in the narrative and in the Johannine church (chap. 11). Martha becomes the paradigm for faith for the community when she proclaims that Jesus is the Messiah. This compelling evidence for a unique, gender-inclusive community gains strength when compared with the synoptic accounts, which place Peter in the central, strategic place in the narrative that also identifies his important role in church leadership. The Johannine community, however, places Martha, not Peter, in the center of their narrative, allowing her confession to be heard, and positioning her as a leader in their church.

This discovery becomes even more striking when John's Gospel is compared with 1 Timothy. Although both books were written concurrently (around 90), and both communities of faith share the same first-century culture, the ethos of the two churches is vastly different. First Timothy describes a community where Mary, Martha, and the Samaritan woman would have been most uncomfortable. In 1 Timothy, leadership for women is impossible; in the Gospel of John, women leaders are encouraged.

While maintaining diversity in membership and theology and advocating an egalitarian community, the Johannine community, without apology, makes exclusive claims for Christ.

For this community, Jesus is God. No gray lines or fuzzy edges exist on this position. Jesus says and the community affirms, "I am the way, and the truth, and the life. No one comes to the Father except through me" (14:6). How can an exclusive position emerge from such an inclusive community, where anyone is welcome, divergent views are honored (even recorded in their document), and women (including a Samaritan) can be leaders?

A knowledge of the larger community is essential for understanding this crucial question. The church's confession, in any era, is never formed in isolation. A conflict always stands somewhere in the shadows. For the Johannine church, it is the synagogue. Although the synagogue has been their home from the beginning, around the middle of the 80s, the Johannine church is expelled (9:22; 12:42; 16:2) because of the radical understanding of Jesus. Before 70, Judaism contained various sects and movements. After the destruction of the temple, however, the rules change, and their positions are concretized. Deviants from orthodoxy are no longer allowed, and the Johannine community is expelled. The community struggles to maintain its understanding of Jesus while surrounded by opposition. The *logia* of Jesus are remembered, "I am the way, and the truth, and the life." The community finds solidarity and identity in the exclusive position.

The community also faces opposition from Roman authorities. No longer protected by the freedom afforded to the Jewish tradition, the Romans see an opportunity to persecute Christians during the late first century. Persons of the Johannine community face these external fears and tighten their position. They believe that Jesus is God, not the emperor. They will not recant, even if they are thrown out of their mother tradition and persecuted by the government.

The Portrait of the Reader

Your face belongs in this Gospel. As you read, who are you? Are you Thomas, who needs to touch before he can believe? Are you Nicodemus, content to remain a secret believer?

Perhaps you identify with the crowds who believe only if they can receive some miraculous sign. Where is your portrait in this vast canvas of Light and people?

I have known that my face belongs in the Fourth Gospel for a long time. I am there, by the well, engaged in theological debate with Jesus. At times, I am Mary Magdalene, the one who is surprised by the Resurrected Lord and then goes to tell others. Sometimes, I am the angry Martha, enraged that my own timetable would be overlooked, finally realizing that God's calendar is not like my own.

I *know* that this Gospel engages the reader. While serving as a missionary in Taiwan, I made a difficult but important decision to return to the States and study the Bible in graduate school. By 1981, I had seen enough of the hurdles for Baptist women who felt called to serve the church. I had already been refused ordination once. I had been told that I was a daughter of Satan several times because I felt called by God to serve the church. I had been asked to sit down and not lead congregational singing because it was not biblical. I was even told by a missionary colleague that God would not hear my prayers unless I prayed them through my husband, and on and on.

I was having great difficulty putting all the pieces together. On one hand, I knew that God had called me to the ministry. While living through this struggle, I tried to analyze that call through the pillars of our faith—experience, tradition, and scripture. In my tradition, personal experience is an important and valid part of hearing God's call. I had the experience to substantiate my call. But on the other hand, tradition had said "No." In 1981, I knew of no other Baptist women preachers. In fact, I was the first woman I ever heard preach a sermon. I inquired of the third pillar of our Baptist understanding of call, scripture. I was stumped! I had been raised in a conservative Baptist home, and the Bible was very important. People around me were saying that the Bible prohibits women from serving the church. With stinging phrases like pellets discharged from a B-B gun, interpreters from the church would say, "Paul says that a woman should be quiet in the church . . . should not usurp man's authority . . . not to seek leadership roles."

103

I was weary and greatly perplexed. One afternoon, in our Chinese apartment on Wo-Lon Street in Taipei, Taiwan, I prayed to God, "I must find out what this Bible is really saying. If I search the Scriptures and find that my call is not validated, I will find another job flipping hamburgers or selling real estate. If my call is there, I will give my life to serving you." In that moment, I made the decision to go back to the Southern Baptist Theological Seminary in Louisville, Kentucky, to see if I could discover what the Bible really did say about women.

I returned to the States and enrolled in seminary as planned. I began the study of the New Testament so that I could discover once and for all if my call was a valid one. I began reading the Gospel of John over and over. I enrolled in Ph.D. seminars on John's Gospel. I decided to write a dissertation on the Fourth Gospel. Somewhere along the way—I can no longer remember the actual day or hour—I found it! I found what I was looking for. I saw my own face within the pages of this Gospel. I was there at the well with Jesus. Oh, I did not have the same matrimonial history. I did not know what it was to have had five marriages end in divorce, but I knew what it was like to be an outcast. I understood what it was like to be marginalized in one's own religious tradition.

I read the story. I saw that Jesus cared enough to talk theology with a woman. I had been overlooked many times in conversations where men were present. At our commissioning service, I remember a denominational leader clasping the hand of my husband to offer his blessing and never once looking in my direction. I remember dinners with colleagues, where I would find myself in the kitchen cleaning dishes while the men talked theology in the dining room. And here in these pages, Jesus is standing by a well in the heat of the day talking theology with a woman—with me!

Then comes the best part. He not only talks with her, he gives her a chance at a new life, a life in which she will not be thirsty again. At the end of the conversation, the woman leaves, perhaps due to the scorn of the disciples. She does not go back to her broken life. Rather, she goes into the city, where all her friends and relatives reside, and she tells them about her encounter. (You could consider this story as the first commissioning service of a female home missionary.) Many people believe because of the woman's testimony. Jesus does not say, "You cannot go tell because the tradition forbids it." Nor does he say, "You may go only if you work with the children and it does not require an official blessing." Rather, Jesus tells the disciples, the same ones who shunned the woman but lacked the courage to vocalize their opposition, that a woman has already planted the Samaritan soil. The disciples are to go and reap what she has sown. Jesus blesses her ministry!

My face belongs on the canvas. My name is to be added to that large roll call of people whose lives have been changed because the Light has come. The Light arrives, and people are not the same. World views are shattered; old paradigms shift; traditional relationships are reconsidered; people are saved because of the powerful portrait of Jesus in the Gospel of John. Arise, shine for *your* Light has come.

Notes

[1]Quoted by E. Haenchen, *John 1*, Hermeneia—A Critical and Historical Commentary on the Bible (Philadelphia: Fortress Press, 1984) 24.

[2]Lynn Miller, "The Portraits of Christ in the Four Gospels," an unpublished paper and slide presentation presented as a requirement in the New Testament Introduction Class, October 1988, Union Theological Seminary, Richmond VA.

[3]Daniel Boorstin, *The Creators* (New York: Random House, 1992) 522.

[4]Ibid., 524.

[5]I am greatly indebted to Alan Culpepper and his insights into this Gospel. We have spent a great deal of time talking about this Gospel in the classroom, in our homes, and in the church. I write this chapter aware that I have unconsciously claimed many of his original ideas as my own. No longer am I sure who owns them. For this reason, I need to ask that you read the source of many of my better thoughts in Culpepper's *The Anatomy of the Fourth Gospel* (Philadelphia: Fortress Press, 1983).

[6]The encounter in chapter 3 does not suggest any change in Nicodemus' life. We do not know if he truly believes in what he has heard. We do see Nicodemus coming to Jesus' defense in front of his colleagues, the chief priests and Pharisees in 7:50-51, which suggests that his fear has been replaced by boldness. Nicodemus also risks being seen when he appears at Jesus' tomb bringing expensive burial spices in 19:39-42.

[7]Linda McKinnish Bridges, "John 4," *Interpretation* 48 (April 1994): 173-76.

[8]J. L. Martyn, *History and Theology of the Fourth Gospel*, 2d rev. ed. (Nashville: Abingdon Press, 1979); Raymond Brown, *The Community of the Beloved Disciple: The Life, Loves, and Hates of an Individual Church in New Testament Times* (New York: Paulist Press, 1979); R. Alan Culpepper, *The Johannine School: An Evaluation of the Nature of Ancient Schools* (Missoula MT: Scholars Press, 1975); and Richard Cassidy, *John's Gospel in New Perspective* (Maryknoll NY: Orbis Books, 1993).

[9]Raymond Brown, "Role of Women in the Fourth Gospel," *Theological Studies*, 36 (1975) 688-99; Sandra M. Schneiders, "Women in the Fourth Gospel and the Role of Women in the Contemporary Church," *Biblical Theology Bulletin* 12 (1982) 34-45.

For Further Reading

Culpepper, Alan. "The Gospel of John," *The Books of the Bible*. New York: Charles Scribner's Sons, 1988.

_____. *The Anatomy of the Gospel of John*. Philadelphia: Fortress Press, 1983.

_____. "Synthesis and Schism in the Johannine Community and the Southern Baptist Convention," *Perspectives in Religious Studies* 13, 1 (Spring 1980): 1-20.

Duke, Paul. *Irony of the Fourth Gospel*. Atlanta: John Knox Press, 1985.

Talbert, Charles. *Reading John: A Literary and Theological Commentary on the Fourth Gospel and the Johannine Epistles*. New York: The Crossroad Publishing Co., Inc., 1992.

Who Is Jesus Christ, Anyway?

The new Christian stood in front of the sanctuary, preparing to be baptized. The water in the baptismal pool had been warming all afternoon. The baptismal hymn had been sung. And now, as was this church's custom, the baptismal candidate was asked to stand in front of the pulpit and to describe his conversion experience, or to "testify" as it was called. This baptismal candidate, however, was different. This was not a young twelve-year-old coming to the age of accountability, nor was this a repentent middle-aged person. Mr. McDuff Dixon was ninety-six years old, walked with a cane, spoke in a weak but tender voice, and had a face so fragile that his tears glistened as they ran down his cheeks.

Earlier that week at the dinner table, Dad had announced that Mr. Dixon was going to be baptized on Sunday evening, and Mom and I shrieked with horror, not at the thought of a new convert, of course, but at the prospect of my pastor Dad and her young husband being responsible for baptizing (by immersion, of course) a ninety-six-year-old man. "What if Dad dropped him as he was dipping him? What if Mr. Dixon were to fall or slip from Dad's arm?" We thought to ourselves. As a young ten-year-old, I wanted a front-row seat that night. As I sat through the hymns, I prayed that Dad would not drop Mr. Dixon in the baptismal water. And then Mr. Dixon began to speak.

He told the church that night how he had been down by the barn all alone one afternoon, when suddenly he began to remember a sermon preached by a traveling evangelist, Baxter McClendon, known as "Cyclone Mac," some eighty years ago. As a sixteen-year-old boy, Dixon had attended a revival meeting in South Carolina, where the fiery evangelist preached a sermon titled, "Who Is Jesus, Anyway?" That afternoon down by the barn, while Mr. Dixon was remembering the sermon, something happened. The Jesus that the preacher had talked about some eighty years ago became real to him, right then, right there as he fed the hogs in the South Carolina sun. This ninety-six-year-old man who had not been to church in eighty years encountered the Living Christ, down by the barn.

He left the revival meeting that night eighty years ago intending never to bother with that "church stuff" anymore, and he had been successful, until that afternoon down by the barn. Dixon remembered his feelings from that night, "This Jesus stuff couldn't be real. It demanded too much. I would have to quit my drinking and smoking, and I couldn't imagine living like that, so I cut out of that meeting like a wild man, and never returned to a service ever again." He had not bothered with faith until that afternoon by the barn when he learned that Jesus Christ was real, not just a figment of some emotional preacher's imagination.

From a camp meeting in the low country of South Carolina to a barn on a sunny afternoon some eighty years later, the words, "Who is Jesus, anyway?" remained in Mr. Dixon's consciousness. This time he could not walk away, and he gave his life to Jesus Christ. His commitment was so intense that he wanted to be baptized and belong to the church even in the last few years of his life. Before he was baptized that night, he remarked that he had finally answered Cyclone Mac's question and could respond by saying that Jesus Christ was the Lord of his life. I will never forget this man, nor the question that haunted him for eighty years: "Who is this Jesus, anyway?"

As this book comes to a close, it is appropriate to ask the same question, "Who is this Jesus, anyway?" It is a question that remains central to the New Testament and for the communities of faith who produced the writings. The communities of faith belonging to the four evangelists, Mark, Matthew, Luke, and John, asked the same question, and the narratives were written as a response.

The response given by the Gospel narratives in the middle of the first century was not the first time the question had been asked, however. Jesus had asked his own disciples the same question: "Who do you say that I am?" While walking one day to Caesarea, Jesus asked, "Who do people say that I am?" The disciples repeated some of the conversations that they had been hearing on the streets and in the marketplace. They responded to Jesus by saying, "Some say you are John the Baptist; and others say that you are Elijah or one of the prophets." Those repeated, secondhand answers were insufficient for Jesus. He said, "But I want to know who do *you* say that I am" (Mark 8:27-29).

It is a personal question that demands a personal response. One cannot read ahead of time, as a student would prepare for an exam. One cannot mindlessly repeat well-worn phrases from ancient texts or tradition. The christological debates of the church from earlier centuries cannot be used as recitation material when this personal question is asked. Even the finest scholarly discussions regarding the nature of Christ lack potency when the question is posed to you personally. The meaning of Jesus is foundationally an existential question. You must answer it yourself. Church confessions will help you to formulate your response. Sermons will assist you, as well. The Gospel stories, which record their memories of Jesus, will also aid your response. But in the final analysis, the answer is yours. Who do *you* think Jesus is?

The Gospel narratives were written as the community wrestled with the question. The church continued to struggle through the centuries in heated council debates at Nicea, Constantinople, and Chalcedon. Group consensus was only temporary, momentarily recorded in a confessional document, only to be reconsidered at the next council meeting.

While words were being formulated into christological confessional statements, ancient visual artists were painting

111

representations of Jesus Christ in the four Gospels. The church was not content with mere words, but also wanted to see visual responses to the christological question. The four Gospel narratives and their christological focus were represented by visual images. These symbols, a lion, a human face, an ox, and an eagle, borrowed from Ezekiel 1:10, represented Mark, Matthew, Luke, and John, respectively, and illuminated ancient manuscripts, frescoes, mosaics, pulpits, and crosses. Mark's Gospel was represented by a lion, since lions roar in deserted places. Matthew's Gospel is remembered by the human face of Jesus, because of the genealogy in the first chapter. The ox represented Luke's Gospel, which begins with the story of the priestly office of Zechariah. The ox symbolized the office of priest in the Hebrew Bible. The eagle signified the Gospel of John ascending to lofty heights. The four symbols came to signify, as Richard Burridge put it, that "Jesus was born as a man, sacrificed like an ox, rose again triumphant like a lion, and ascended like an eagle, extending his wings to protect his people."[1]

Art history, however, notes that even these symbols lacked a stable interpretation through time. For example, Irenaeus, bishop of Lyons, writing at the end of the second century, wrote that the lion symbol described the Jesus in John, while the eagle was most applicable to Mark's Gospel. Later around 400, Jerome, Bible scholar and translator, wrote that Jesus was best visualized as an eagle in John and a lion in Mark. Some artists, such as the Celtic craftsmen who produced *The Book of Durrow* around 650–675 CE, saw Jesus as an eagle in Mark rather than a lion. Artists continued to change the early designs and interpretation, opting for a rather stylized face for Matthew and an eagle with folded, rather than outstretched, wings for John. Around 750 CE, however, all four symbols were combined in *The Book of Kells*, now housed in Trinity College, Dublin, Ireland. This particular manuscript illumination carefully arranged all four symbols around the central figure of Christ in a composite picture.

Perhaps it is this composite picture, or montage, where the church's portrait of Jesus can best be illustrated. This composite does not isolate any image over another and chooses to paint all four symbols in harmony with the primary figure of Christ. To isolate a single visual representation minimizes the full effect of the composite portrait. To give only a one-dimensional view of Christ as depicted through one symbol ignores the other three attributes, and the power of the portrait is significantly diminished.

And so it is with the Gospel narratives. Frank Colquhoun describes the church's portraits in this manner:

> The picture offered by each of the Gospels is a distinctive one, with its own clearly drawn features. That is why we need all four pictures and cannot afford to dispense with any of them. Every Gospel in turn adds something of value to our total understanding of the person of Christ and of the the work he came to do for our salvation. . . . And it is only as we keep the whole portrait in view that we shall come to see the whole Christ.[2]

In order to understand each Gospel, I have isolated the christological portraits, maximizing their distinctions by pointing to the particular features painted by the various communities of faith in the first century and their unique expressions of the faith. The earliest portrait, produced by the community surrounding Mark's Gospel, announces that Jesus is the Son of God. In this relational way, Jesus appears as one who is strong in weakness, able to calm a storm yet unable to preserve his own life. In Matthew, Jesus is the teaching Messiah, dressed in Jewish rabbinic garments giving instructions for daily living. In Luke, Jesus sits at table with outcasts and sinners, engaging freely in conversation, all the while breaking religious conventions in a most subtle yet subversive manner. In John, Jesus' hands are outstretched as he welcomes sinners home, saves those who are lost, and brings those from the margins back to the center while simultaneously changing their lives.

These portraits are not to be seen in isolation, however, but as a composite or a christological montage. This Jesus is

not just a humble revolutionary nor a maverick with a strong
social consciousness. This Jesus is more than just an ethereal
imaginative spirit who glides into the room, heals some folk,
then flees to some unknown crevice in history. This is God
made flesh in multiple ways. Just as the human personality
contains more than one attribute, so does Jesus Christ reveal
more than one portrait. The irony is, however, that in order to
see the whole, one must appreciate the parts. And the parts,
the four portraits of Jesus in the Gospels, are particular representations of four communties of faith. Jesus is the Son of God
in Mark, who teaches in Matthew, eats at table in Luke, and
saves people in John. Yet, in order to understand the fullness
of Jesus Christ, the christological montage is necessary.

But that still is not enough. Even if you have read every
page, even every sentence, of this book carefully and remain
convinced of the literary portraits of Jesus as I have interpreted them from the four Gospels, you still cannot adequately
answer Cyclone Mac's question: "Who is Jesus Christ,
anyway?" You have been viewing other people's portraits of
Christ, through the eyes of the Markan community, for example, and not your own. Although the Scriptures as the word of
God mediate revelation to us, that revelation cannot only
reside in a first-century container, nor can this Jesus. Tom
Long describes it this way:

> In a deeper sense, not only is Jesus not a middle class guy
> who drove a Mitsubishi, he also refuses to lie still on the
> examining table while historians conduct an autopsy. He is a
> living presence who spills over the dam built to separate the
> past from the present.[3]

The experience of the risen Christ is tantamount to any
historical reconstruction or literary portrait. To experience the
painting, we must be there. The response to a beautiful work
of art is more than knowing its history or even its contemporary historical context. A response to art is made even when
the surrounding information is missing. You stand there in the
gallery, admire the work, and something inside of you flutters.

You see color and shades of light that cannot be analyzed nor even fully discussed. This visceral response is not diminished simply because you cannot describe it nor appropriately label it. The response remains. You are moved. Something inside of you changes. And so it is when you see Jesus' portrait for yourself, even moreso.

Your image of Jesus matters. How you think about Jesus affects how you understand your faith. Marcus Borg says that "our image of Jesus affects our perception of the Christian life in two ways: it gives shape to the Christian life, and it can make Christianity credible or incredible."[4] It is significant to ask yourself, "Who is Jesus?" I cannot answer it for you, only offer some insights from history. It is now up to you.

Even after all the communities of faith have laid down their paint brushes, the voices of the council leaders have hushed, and the mosaics have been destroyed by wind and age, the portrait of Jesus remains, but only as an interesting relic from the past. You are the one who now must decide the colors and the shape, the position of the head, and the angle of the chin. You must determine the shades of light and the surrounding context. Paint Jesus as Friend, Savior, God. The images are many, just paint. As you paint, God's Spirit will reveal the presence of Christ to you. Who is this Jesus Christ, anyway?

Notes

[1]Richard A. Burridge, *Four Gospels, One Jesus?* (Grand Rapids: Wm. B. Eerdmans Publishing Co., 1994) 28.

[2]Frank Colquhoun, *Four Portraits of Jesus: Christ in the Gospels* (Downers Grove IL: InterVarsity Press, 1984) 4.

[3]Tom Long, "Stand Up, Stand Up for (the Historical) Jesus," *Theology Today* (April 1995): 4.

[4]Marcus Borg, *Meeting Jesus Again for the First Time* (San Francisco: Harper, 1994) 2.

ALL THE BIBLE

ALL THE BIBLE SERIES DESCRIPTION

AREA	TITLE*
Genesis–Deuteronomy	From Creation to Lawgiving
Former Prophets	Israel's Rise and Decline
Latter Prophets, excluding Postexilic	God's Servants, the Prophets
Poetry, Wisdom Literature	The Testimony of Poets and Sages
Exilic, Postexilic Books	The Exile and Beyond
The Four Gospels	The Church's Portraits of Jesus
Acts of the Apostles, Epistles of Paul	The Church's Mission to the Gentiles
Hebrews–Revelation	The Church as a Pilgrim People

*Titles Subject to Change